# WOMAN OVERBOARD

*A Musical Comedy*

*by*

**Jack Sharkey & Dave Reiser**

S A M U E L   F R E N C H ,   I N C .

25 West 45th Street     New York 10036
7623 Sunset Boulevard     Hollywood 90046
*London*           *Toronto*

"WOMAN OVERBOARD" had its world premiere on May 7, 1977 at the Maryville Academy Auditorium, DesPlaines, Illinois, via the MUSIC ON STAGE, Inc., Players, with the following cast:

PEGGY TREMAYNE ...................Venus Miller

MADGE TREMAYNE ..................Gail Yokubinas

HARRY TREMAYNE ......................Pete Piper

ANGELICA BOSTICK ..................Jan Di Cosola

CLARENCE BOSTICK ...................Jim Curren

DEBBY TREMAYNE ................Kathy Lubinski

LORENZO LA JOLLA ...............Bob Mangelsdorf

OFFICER.................................Jim Shrum

STEWARD .......................Rick Stuhlmann

WAITER ...........................Joe Schaedal

PHARMACIST ...................Marge Mangelsdorf

Dancers .....Sue Lukaszewski, Debbie Zdunek, Marge Mangelsdorf

Passengers & Natives.............Anne Marie Conard, Marguerite Dietrich, Myrle Donovan, Pat Spilotro, Sharon McManus, Toni Higgins, Gail Yokubinas, Jim Shrum, Rick Stuhlmann, Joe Schaedal

Choreography .........................Toni Higgins

Vocal Director and Accompanist.....Jeanne Stillmann

Entire Production under the direction of Ed Sauer

3

ACT ONE

Scene 1) The Tremayne home

2) A boarding pier

3) The Tremayne stateroom on the "Fiesta Queen"

4) The promenade deck

5) The ship's lounge

6) The ship's dining room

7) The native marketplace on Tumbango

8) The ship's pharmacy

9) Entrance to the ship's ballroom

10) The ship's ballroom

ACT TWO

Scene 1) The Tremayne stateroom

2) All over the Caribbean

3) The Tremayne stateroom

4) A corridor on the ship

5) The ship's bridge and Debby's cabin

6) The lifeboat deck

7) The Tremayne home

# "WOMAN OVERBOARD"

ACT ONE, SCENE ONE

*The Tremayne home, basically the kitchen and living
room areas. Living room has a lounge chair and a
TV, kitchen has usual equipment, and we can see
the back door. It is a comfortable home, inexpen-
sively but tastefully furnished.*

*At curtain-rise, the open refrigerator door hides* PEGGY
TREMAYNE; *when we see her, she will be an attractive mature woman in a housedress, happily
preparing dinner with whatever she takes from the
refrigerator and brings to the work surface beside
the sink. As she works there, back door opens and*
MADGE TREMAYNE *enters. She is about* PEGGY'S
*age, but is dressed well in casual chic, and has ob-
viously never done a lick of housework in her life.*

MADGE. Peggy, I've got the most exciting news!

PEGGY. Oh, hi, Madge! My, that's a pretty outfit.

MADGE. It ought to be — I paid a pretty penny for it.

PEGGY. Listen, can you beat these eggs while I find
the celery? Harry will be home any minute, and he likes
his dinner on time.

MADGE. (*picking up egg and studying it*) Do I break
this open first, or what?

PEGGY. Oh, Madge, don't you ever do any cooking at
all?

7

MADGE. Good gravy, no! If I set foot in our kitchen, the cook would give notice! But let me tell you my news —

HARRY. (*off*) Peg? I'm home! (HARRY TREMAYNE, *a nice, ordinary middle-forties man, enters living room and crosses toward kitchen*)

PEGGY. Hi, honey! Dinner will be just a few more minutes.

(*as* HARRY *enters kitchen*)

Why don't you watch some television and put your feet up?

HARRY. Okay, hon — Oh, hi, Madge. How's my favorite sister-in-law?

MADGE. Harry, that joke was stale at my wedding. I'm your *only* sister-in-law!

HARRY. (*produces bouquet from behind back*) For my favorite wife!

PEGGY. Oh, darling, how nice! What are they?

HARRY. *Lathyrus Latifolius.*

MADGE. Didn't he used to run the Roman Empire?

HARRY. (*amicably*) "Sweet Peas" to you! (*exits to living room*)

PEGGY. (*putting flowers into vase*) Wasn't that nice of Harry!

MADGE. Peg, honey, he *does* run a *flower* nursery! Now, if he'd brought you *candy* —

PEGGY. I'd get fat, and *then* where would we be!

MADGE. If you'll pardon my asking — where are you *now*?

PEGGY. Right where I want to be. In my own kitchen, in my own house, fixing dinner for my very own man. What else has life to offer?

MADGE. How about a two-week, all-expense-paid Caribbean cruise?

(*when* PEGGY *laughs this notion away:*)

What's so funny? I know for a fact you enter six dozen contests a year! ''No purchase necessary — just put your name and address on a plain piece of paper —''

PEGGY. Madge, I don't do that for me, I do it for Harry! Men get — oh — restless. They need a change now and then. *Listen* — (*calls toward living room*) Harry — how was your day — ?

HARRY. (*seated in lounge chair before TV*) Same old grind. Ulcer City all the way — survival of the fittest! (*sings*)
It's great to get home from that rat race.
One day you're a bull, and the next you're a bear.
It's dog-eating-dog, each day in and day out.
It's a regular jungle out there!
Some days I'm too chicken to fight it.
A leopard just can't change his spots, I declare.
I spend ev'ry coffee break dining on crow.
It's a regular jungle out there!
(*Music continues under following, which is spoken rhythmically, but not sung.*)

PEGGY. You see what I mean, Madge?

MADGE. I do, yessiree! You need a vacation!

PEGGY. No, that's not for me — (*sings*)
It's wonderful just to be
An average housewife like me!
To care for my very own man
The best way I know or I can.
To cook and to wash and to sew
And to clean. And it's lovely to know
This way I may impart
The love that I feel in my heart!
(*Music continues under rhythmic speaking as before.*)

MADGE.
Peg, you've gone bananas,
No ifs and no buts!

PEGGY.
Oh, Madge, don't be silly.
    MADGE.
This setup is nuts!
Your mind must be cracking
To rave on like that!
    PEGGY.
No, your logic's lacking
The simple fact that —
                    (*sings in overlap-duet with* HARRY:)
            HARRY.                          PEGGY.

| HARRY. | PEGGY. |
|---|---|
| It's great to get home from that rat race. | It's wonderful just to be |
| One day you're a bull, and the next you're a bear. | An average housewife like me! |
| It's dog-eating-dog, each day in and day out. | To care for my very own man |
| It's a regular jungle out there! | The best way I know or I can. |
| Some days I'm too chicken to fight it. | To cook and to wash and to sew |
| A leopard just can't change his spots, I declare. | And to clean. And it's lovely to know |
| I spend ev'ry coffee break | This way |
| Dining on crow. | I may impart |
| It's a regular | The love that I |
| Jungle out there! | Feel in my heart! |

    MADGE. (*grimly shakes her head as song ends*)
Lawrence Welk would be crazy about you two! Childhood
sweethearts, domestic bliss, and pass the Pepto-Bismol!

    PEGGY. Okay, Madge. You're right. A break in
routine would be fun. But my life's tied up in Harry's.
What he does, I do. Where he goes, I go.

    MADGE. That's absolutely perfect! (*whips envelope
from pocket, hands it to* PEGGY)

PEGGY. What's this?

MADGE. Two first-class tickets on the Fiesta Queen, all expenses paid. It's only the most luxurious cruise ship in the Caribbean. You'll love it!

PEGGY. Oh, Madge, I couldn't—!

MADGE. Good grief, girl, this isn't a *gift*! There's a string attached.

PEGGY. (*shakes head*) Isn't that just like your Henry!

MADGE. *Henry* doesn't *know* about this! He'd *never* do this for his *brother*!

PEGGY. You're not making sense—whose tickets *are* these?

MADGE. (*patiently*) Mine and Henry's. Everything's booked under *our* names, see? But Henry thinks I'm taking the tickets back for a refund.

PEGGY. Then why aren't you?

MADGE. Because of Debby. Her heart's been set on this trip for months. And now, to all at once tell her she can't go because her father has to go to a gynecologists' convention—! I don't have the heart.

PEGGY. (*thinks she follows*) Oh, you're going to a convention instead of on the cruise!

MADGE. Me? Don't be ridiculous! Did you ever attend a gynecologists' convention? Every time a man looks you up and down, you feel you have to pay him!

PEGGY. But—if you don't get the refund—?

MADGE. All part of the plan, honey. Madge is staying at home-sweet-home, but Henry thinks she's going to Las Vegas, where she will proceed to lose all the money she was refunded. Isn't that brilliant?

PEGGY. Not quite. How do you explain Debby's Caribbean suntan afterwards?

MADGE. Oh, Henry thinks *she's* still going. Alone.

PEGGY. Alone? Madge. Debby is only eighteen years old! You'd send a child like that on a Caribbean cruise with no one to look after her?!

MADGE. (*taps the envelope* PEGGY *holds*) Nobody except Aunt Peggy and Uncle Harry.

PEGGY. Oh!

MADGE. Exactly. That's the string attached. Take care of my little girl.

PEGGY. Well . . . I guess . . . maybe if I work on Harry for awhile . . . and don't mention his brother Henry . . . tell him I won one of those contests I'm always entering—

MADGE. How fast can you work?

PEGGY. When does the ship sail?

MADGE. Noon tomorrow.

PEGGY. *Noon tomorr*—?! (*remembers* HARRY, *lowers voice*) Madge, I couldn't! There are the children—Harry's business—!

MADGE. Harry can turn the flower shop over to his assistant, you can cancel the newspaper with a phone call, and your kids can move in with our mutual mother-in-law. It'd serve her right.

PEGGY. But Madge—noon tomorrow—I can't possibly—!

MADGE. Of course you can. It's perfectly simple!

PEGGY. What would I *wear* on a cruise?!

MADGE. As little as possible.

PEGGY. I mean *I* don't own anything suitable for—

MADGE. No problem. You and I are the same size—more or less—and I'm all packed—and we're both named "Margaret," so the monograms should be okay . . . so you just take *my* luggage, and— Oh! I nearly forgot! Don't let Harry take his hat off during the trip! He can't let anyone see his hair!

PEGGY. Why can't he?

MADGE. (*again explaining patiently*) Because *he's* traveling under *Henry's* name, and Henry is bald as a *grape,* so—

PEGGY. Harry's traveling under—?

MADGE. Well, if you're traveling as *me*, naturally *Harry* has to travel as—

PEGGY. Madge, not so fast—who said I was traveling as you?!

MADGE. Peg, darling, you *have* to! If the eligible men on the ship find out Debby's only with an aunt and uncle, who knows *what* might happen! Parents are something else again.

PEGGY. Madge, you call this *simple*?!

MADGE. What could be simpler?

PEGGY. But it's crazy—!

MADGE. *Life* is crazy! Don't fight it—relax and enjoy it! (*starts for door*) Now hurry and start deceiving your husband, I've got to help Debby finish packing.

PEGGY. *Debby*—that's *another* thing—how do I explain Debby coming *with* us?

MADGE. You'll think of something. Harry's crazy about Debby. He'll buy it.

PEGGY. But Madge—!

(*But* MADGE *is gone;* PEGGY *stands irresolute, and at that moment,* HARRY *rises and turns off TV in living room.*)

HARRY. (*starting toward kitchen*) Peg—? Dinner ready yet—?

PEGGY. What dinner? Oh! Dinner! A—a few more minutes, honey . . .

HARRY. (*en route*) What's taking you so long—?

PEGGY. (*doesn't even hear; staring at envelope in her hand, she begins to sing, slowly, musingly:*)
Maybe we could do it . . .
There's not that much to it . . .
With some ingenuity . . .
We could leave plebeian
Things behind, and flee un—
To the Caribbean Sea . . . !

HARRY. (*just catching this as he enters kitchen*)
*Where*—?!
PEGGY. (*whirls on him, clutches his arms, and as
music goes suddenly up-tempo, continues excitedly:*)
The kids could move in with your mother!
Some neighbor could pick up the mail!
The dog we could leave with another!
Then off to the ship and away we sail!
　　HARRY. *What*—?!
　　PEGGY. (*thoughtfully heavenward*)
Do we dare to try it?
Can I justify it?
Is it impropriety?
　(*as* HARRY *almost speaks, places fingers on his lips*)
Save your reasons why
It's wrong till you and I
Are under some papaya tree!
　　HARRY. *Just a minute*—!
　　PEGGY. (*clutches his hands fervently*)
When decisions are up for adoption
And there isn't much time to delay,
We have only one possible option—
　　　(*starts towing him out of kitchen toward hall*)
Let's head out
And fight about it on the way!
(*and as they vanish, a sea-backdrop descends and
　　screens them from sight, as a pair of boarding-pier
　　projections slide in from right and left, and we are
　　in:*)


ACT ONE, SCENE TWO


*The gangplank of the "Fiesta Queen" is just visible at
extreme left. A ship's* OFFICER *sits at a small table*

*at the foot of the gangplank. From right,* CLAR-
ENCE BOSTICK *enters, followed by* ANGELICA
BOSTICK, *a handsome rich widow in her sixties; she
carries luggage, a pick and shovel, and a pith
helmet; he is emptyhanded. They pause at* OFFI-
CER'S *table.*

CLARENCE. Clarence Bostick and baggage.
ANGELICA. I resent that.
CLARENCE. And mother.
OFFICER. Do you have anything to declare before
boarding?
ANGELICA. I'm coming down with a headache.
OFFICER. I didn't mean that, Mrs. Bostick.
ANGELICA. Well, I did! (*drops gear*) Clarence, I
refuse to stir another foot with all this junk. We are cer-
tainly rich enough to afford a porter.
CLARENCE. A porter only comes with a railroad
train, Mother.
ANGELICA. I don't care if he comes with the whole
Union Pacific, I'll pay him anything!
OFFICER. Steward!
　　　(STEWARD *descends gangplank*)
Will you kindly take this—uh—equipment on board?
STEWARD. (*gathering it up*) Where does it go?
ANGELICA. Over the side, for all I care! (*flexes
fingers to restore circulation*)
CLARENCE. You know our usual cabin, Steward.
OFFICER. (*before* STEWARD *can quite start up
gangplank*) Oh, just a moment—Mister Bostick, I'm
afraid you don't have your usual cabin this trip. It's
been booked by a Doctor and Mrs. Tremayne.
ANGELICA. But I am worth sixty million dollars!
How dare they book my cabin!
OFFICER. (*tactfully*) I'm extremely sorry, Mrs.
Bostick, but—well—it *is* first-come-first-served—

ANGELICA. You mean they're on board?

OFFICER. Well, no, but—

ANGELICA. Then we've come first! Steward, our usual cabin! (*starts off*)

OFFICER. Mrs. Bostick—!

ANGELICA. (*stops, looks him up and down*) Are you married?

OFFICER. Uh—why do you ask—?

ANGELICA. Because if you're not . . . you may call me "Angelica"!

CLARENCE. (*trying to explain her flirtatiousness*) Mother's not married, either.

STEWARD. What does that make *you*?

CLARENCE. She is a *widow*!

STEWARD. Begging your pardon, sir—I thought she might be one of them modern swingers.

CLARENCE. (*ruefully*) As a matter of fact—she is!

ANGELICA. Can we *please* go to our cabin?!

OFFICER. (*to* STEWARD) Cabin one-oh-one, B-Deck.

(STEWARD *starts up gangplank with gear.*)

ANGELICA. B-Deck, indeed! Young man, the owner of this steamship line shall hear of this!

CLARENCE. (*as they start up gangplank after* STEWARD) Mother, *you* are the owner of this steamship line!

ANGELICA. (*with inane determination*) In that case, *I* haven't heard the *end* of this!

(*She storms proudly up and out of sight with* CLARENCE *tagging resignedly after her; as they vanish,* DEBBY TREMAYNE *enters, right; she is a perfectly lovely 18-year-old; she glances about, hesitates, then moves shyly up to the* OFFICER'S *table.*)

DEBBY. Excuse me—but—have the Tremaynes checked in with you yet?

OFFICER. Not yet, Miss—are you sailing with them or just seeing them off?

DEBBY. Oh, sailing. In my own cabin, isn't that neat? Oh, but I suppose you're used to this sort of thing. (CLARENCE *reappears on gangplank, descends to pier.*) But I'm really excited. I've never been abroad before.

CLARENCE. (*while scanning pier for something, not looking at her*) What were you, a cocker spaniel?

DEBBY. What—?

CLARENCE. (*paying her no attention, to* OFFICER:) Did you see anything of a small blue overnight bag, Officer? It's very important—it has three of my diamond-bit drills in it.

(*to* DEBBY, *casually showing off*) I'm an archaeologist. I do a lot of boring.

DEBBY. So I've noticed.

(*As he gapes,* DEBBY *spots something off right, starts in that direction, as* ANGELICA *appears on gangplank carrying the overnight bag.*)

ANGELICA. Here it is, Clarence! Now, come on, help me fight for my cabin!

CLARENCE. (*starts up, but continues to stare toward* DEBBY) The nerve of that girl! Did you hear what she said to me?!

ANGELICA. (*hands bag to him*) What did you say to her first?

CLARENCE. (*indignant*) Mother! What makes you think that I—?

ANGELICA. (*interrupts wearily*) Because you *always*!

(*As they exit from view,* HARRY *and* PEGGY *enter right, just as* DEBBY *arrives at that point;* PEGGY *wears an expensive travel suit,* HARRY *wears a large fedora.*)

PEGGY. Debby, darling! Isn't this fun! (*they embrace*)

HARRY. Debby! Hey, it's nice of you to come and see us off!

DEBBY. See you off? Aunt Peggy, didn't you tell him about—

PEGGY. (*quickly*) Harry! Why don't you make sure there's no luggage left on the pier back there with that steward, while I check us in?

HARRY. (*amicably starts off right*) I wouldn't be surprised if there were! Where did you *get* all those bags anyhow? (*dutifully exits*)

DEBBY. Aunt Peggy, why does Uncle Harry think I came to see you off?

PEGGY. I can only feed him one mouthful at a time! It was all I could do to get him into that fedora!

DEBBY. That looks like one of my father's hats—!

PEGGY. For heaven's sake, don't tell that to your uncle! Honey, didn't your mother explain *any* of this to you?

DEBBY. Well—sort of. She said *you'd* explain everything.

PEGGY. Good old Madge!

DEBBY. But why does Uncle Harry—?

PEGGY. Look, I'll fill you in later. Meantime, don't call me "Aunt Peggy" when any strangers are around, and don't call me anything but "Mom" when Harry's not around!

(*As* DEBBY *gapes,* PEGGY *moves to* OFFICER'S *table, quickly, to get it over with before* HARRY'S *return.*)
Hello! Doctor and Mrs. Tremayne and daughter—?

OFFICER. (*checks list*) Ah, yes! Everything's in order. You're in one-oh-one, on A-Deck . . .
(*as* HARRY *re-enters*)
. . . and your daughter is in one-oh-two on B.

DEBBY. (*to* HARRY *as he joins them*) You know, you look good in a hat. I've never seen you in one before.

HARRY. I never owned one before. Your aunt bought it for the trip. She says the salt air is bad for my sinuses.

PEGGY. (*moving hastily from table*) We're all set, darlings, let's go aboard, quick!

OFFICER. (*as they pass him en route to the gangplank*) Oh, excuse me, sir—

HARRY. (*as they pause*) Yes—?

OFFICER. I noticed your occupation on the passenger list, sir, and—

PEGGY. Come on, darlings, I'm dying to see our cabin!

HARRY. Just a minute, honey, the man's trying to say something.

OFFICER. Well—I don't mean to interfere or anything, but—if I were you—on a trip like this—I'd keep my line of work a secret.

HARRY. What in the world for?

OFFICER. A lot of women might start pestering you for free advice, if you know what I mean—?

HARRY. (*blankly*) What's to advise? There are only two things to remember—the live ones need proper drainage, the others need refrigeration.

PEGGY. (*as* OFFICER *gapes, grabs* HARRY'S *arm*) And everybody knows that! (*quickly leads him up gangplank, with* DEBBY *following, and as they vanish, the projections slide off, and the backdrop rises to reveal:*)


ACT ONE, SCENE THREE

*The Tremayne stateroom, the epitome of shipboard magnificence—drapes, carpeting, desk, chairs, double bed, all just gorgeous.* PEGGY, DEBBY *and* HARRY *enter behind* STEWARD, *the women looking about with pleasure,* HARRY *looking about in slack-jawed amazement.*

HARRY. (*after an incredulous pause*) Tell me again about that contest. This isn't a cabin—it's a floating Taj Mahal!

PEGGY. Can I help it if I've got a lucky streak? (*tips* STEWARD) That will be all, thank you.

STEWARD. Thank *you*! I'll go and see about your luggage, now. (*exits*)

HARRY. How much did you give him? He almost salaamed!

PEGGY. Only five dollars.

HARRY. For opening the door?!

PEGGY. Madge says it's customary.

HARRY. *Madge*?! Peg, don't start picking up *her* habits! That sister-in-law of ours tips the *mailman*!

PEGGY. Oh, darling—don't spoil it. Our first real vacation away from the children—? Oh, except for Debby, I mean.

HARRY. (*to* DEBBY) You're coming *with* us?

DEBBY. In my own cabin! Isn't that neat?!

HARRY. (*to* PEGGY) Wait a minute—how can *Debby* be coming on *our* trip?!

PEGGY. (*desperately fast*) She won a contest, too! (*Before* HARRY *can dispute this, there is a rap at door.*) Come in! Come in!

(HARRY *holds his fire as* STEWARD *enters with monogrammed luggage, all expensive-looking.*)

STEWARD. Here are your bags, and the trunk is on its way.

HARRY. We have a *trunk*? Peg—these suitcases—those clothes—where in the world have you been keeping them?

PEGGY. They came with the contest.

STEWARD. What contest?

(*Before* PEGGY *can field this new hazard,* ANGELICA *and* CLARENCE *enter through still-open door.*)

Mrs. Bostick, please! As I've already told you a dozen times—!

DEBBY. Told her what?

ANGELICA. You people seem to have taken my cabin!

HARRY. I knew it was too good to be true.

PEGGY. Now, just a minute—!

ANGELICA. I've sailed on this ship dozens of times, and I *always* have this cabin!

CLARENCE. Mother, I *told* you to make our reservations early!

ANGELICA. Clarence, don't you dare take their part!

HARRY. Steward, just whose cabin *is* this?

STEWARD. Yours, sir. Mrs. Bostick has no claim to it, believe me.

ANGELICA. But I always have this cabin! I had it on this ship's maiden voyage!

DEBBY. Maybe you should have planted a flag.

PEGGY. Debby, that's not good manners.

DEBBY. What about *her* manners?

CLARENCE. Now, listen, young lady—!

ANGELICA. No, Clarence, wait. She's quite right. My manners stink. It's one of the benefits of being rich, you don't have to be polite, too.

HARRY. *I* think *everyone* should be polite!

ANGELICA. Then why haven't you taken off your hat?

PEGGY. Don't, Harry—I think it makes you look distinguished!

HARRY. But my scalp's getting all sweaty. And my sinuses never felt better.

CLARENCE. While you're at it, how's your lumbago?

DEBBY. Now, *look,* tall-dark-and-stuck-up, nobody *asked* you to come in here—!

PEGGY. But *I'm* certainly about to ask you to get the hell *out*! Both of you!

ANGELICA. (*ominously*) People don't *speak* to me like that!

HARRY. (*unimpressed*) *I'm* surprised they speak to you at *all*!

STEWARD. (*ill-at-ease*) Uh—I'll just go and see about that trunk! (*eager to flee Ground Zero, bolts out and shuts door*)

HARRY. Hey, he didn't wait for a tip!

ANGELICA. They never do when there's an argument going on. That's why I argue so much. It saves money.

PEGGY. I got the impression you were wealthy.

ANGELICA. Oh, I am. And not tipping helps me stay that way!

(*despite themselves, the three* TREMAYNES *laugh*) There, that's better. You are all perfectly right. I have terrible manners, and no business being in your cabin. Clarence *told* me my bluff wouldn't work. (*extends hands to* PEGGY) I do beg your pardon. How do you do?

PEGGY. How do you do, Mrs. Bostick. I'm—uh—Margaret Tremayne, and this is my husband Harry . . . oh, and—uh—Debby.

CLARENCE. (*coolly*) I've already had that pleasure.

ANGELICA. Clarence, don't be so icy. Clarence is my son. He's an archaeologist. Every time I send him out to find a young girl, he digs up an old crock!

(*Before* CLARENCE *can defend himself,* STEWARD *re-enters with large wicker basket of lovely flowers and brings them to* PEGGY)

STEWARD. Excuse me, Mrs. Tremayne—these are for you.

PEGGY. Oh, Harry, you shouldn't have!

HARRY. I didn't!

PEGGY. Honestly? Then who—?

DEBBY. (*has found card amid the flowers, reads it aloud*) "To my *hermosa Margarita,* from her adoring Lorenzo." Wow!

PEGGY. But *I* don't know any—?

STEWARD. Captain La Jolla specifically mentioned you by name, Mrs. Tremayne.

ANGELICA. Ah, then you've sailed this ship before! That Lorenzo! He never forgets a torrid romance!

HARRY. A *what*?! Just *who* is Lorenzo La Jolla?!

PEGGY. Harry, darling, I *swear*—!

ANGELICA. I envy you, my dear. I've yearned after Lorenzo for years. A man who looks so much like Fernando Lamas should be horsewhipped!

HARRY. With a name like his, make that a bullwhip. Where can I buy one?

ANGELICA. (*hand on his arm*) If what you suspect is true, and you should need consolation—my cabin is just below this one.

DEBBY. Oh, really? Then it must be right next door to mine!

ANGELICA. (*a hopeful matchmaker*) Did you catch that, Clarence—?

STEWARD. Mrs. Tremayne—will there be any reply to the captain?

HARRY. Yeah! What's Spanish for "How would you like a punch in the nose!"?

(*Ship's whistle blows;* STEWARD *heads for door.*)

STEWARD. That's the all-ashore. I'd better see about your trunk.

(*He exits; whistle blows again;* PEGGY *clutches* HARRY'S *hand as a pulse-beat of music starts in the orchestra;* ALL *will* **sing** *remainder of this scene.*)

PEGGY.
It's happening!
DEBBY.
It's here at last!
HARRY.
I feel it now!
ANGELICA.
The die is cast!
CLARENCE.
We've left the pier—
HARRY.
We're moving out—
PEGGY.
We're free and clear, beyond a doubt!
ALL.
We're feeling delicious and wildly aware that
The time is propitious to gaily declare that—

We're off and away, and we're happy to say
It's a beautiful day for a trip!
The weather is fine, and the air is like wine,
And we're on a divine little ship!
The world is in rhyme, and the future's sublime,
So we haven't the time for dismay!
At worries we'll scoff, for our hearts are aloft
To be finally off and away!
PEGGY.
I hope to find adventures!
HARRY.
With luck I'll get a tan!
ANGELICA.
I'll polish up my dentures,
Then go and catch a man!
CLARENCE.
I'll study native cultures,
And animals and plants

From pinto beans to vultures!
   DEBBY.
Perhaps I'll find romance!
   ALL.
Weeeeeeee're
Off and away, and we're happy to say
It's a beautiful day for a trip!
The weather is fair, and there's wine in the air,
And the itinerary's a pip!

It's very exciting and almost a fright
To go off for a bright holiday!
But worries we'll doff, for our hearts are aloft
To be finally off and away!
   CLARENCE.
The social things that bore me
I'll try to rise above!
   PEGGY.
Enchantment lies before me!
   DEBBY.
Oh, where-oh-where is love?
   HARRY.
The tropic day is slow, but
I do enjoy a nap!
   ANGELICA.
I'll put on something low-cut
And see who I can trap!
   ALL.
Weeeeeeee're
Off and away, and we're happy to say
It's a beautiful day for a trip!
Our past is a blur and we all must concur
That we've given our worries the slip!
We're finally free to be no one but we,
And to find us the fun that is second-to-none—

PEGGY.
Excitement!
HARRY.
A tan!
CLARENCE.
Native customs!
DEBBY/ANGELICA.
A man!
ALL.
With our scruples in grand disarray,
It's lovely to note we're all in the same boat,
And our boat is afloat—
ANGELICA.
And away!
DEBBY.
Away!
PEGGY.
Away!
CLARENCE.
Away!
HARRY.
Away!
ALL. (*a shout of joy*) HURRAY!

(*A backdrop of open deck falls before them, a projection with some deck chairs slides on, and we are into—*)


ACT ONE, SCENE FOUR

*The promenade deck.* STEWARD *enters from right,
starts across, then pauses as Captain* LORENZO LA
JOLLA *enters from left, resplendent in white
uniform with gold braid; he is a man of bronzed*

*Latin handsomeness, and does indeed look exactly
like Fernando Lamas.*

LORENZO. Steward! You delivered the flowers as I re-
quested?

STEWARD. Yes, Captain La Jolla. The lady was much
impressed. However, she said she did not know you, or
why you would send her flowers.

LORENZO. Aha! Was her husband in the room?

STEWARD. Why—yes, he was . . .?

LORENZO. Then what did you *expect* the lady to say?!

STEWARD. Of course! I didn't think! And she certainly did like those flowers! But—I should warn you—her
husband was extremely unpleasant about them.

LORENZO. I do not fear her husband.

STEWARD. He is not a small man.

LORENZO. True, but he has a weak stomach. I shall
simply do what I did the last time my Margarita sailed
with me—steer a course through the roughest possible
seas. Then my Margarita can be in my arms, while her
husband is in his cabin taking Dramamine.

STEWARD. But sir—what if the *other* passengers get
seasick, too?

LORENZO. When I am with *mi hermosa Margarita*—
there *are* no other passengers!

STEWARD. (*shrugs*) You're the captain!

LORENZO. And don't you forget it!

(STEWARD *continues his cross and exits, as* ANGELICA
*and* CLARENCE *enter opposite, he carrying a
folding deck chair;* LORENZO *moves toward her as*
CLARENCE *sets up chair.*)

LORENZO. Ah, it is the beautiful Mrs. Bostick! (*bows
and kisses her hand*)

ANGELICA. Ah, Lorenzo, Lorenzo! Why do you tor-
ture me with empty attentions? When a man tees off,
the least he can do is offer to follow through!

LORENZO. Dear lady, I worship you from afar, as an unworthy pilgrim at an unapproachable shrine!

ANGELICA. You Latins have such a charming way of telling a lady to get lost.

CLARENCE. Mother, your chair is ready, but I forgot your blanket.

ANGELICA. (*moving to chair, where she will sit*) Oh, never mind the blanket, it's warm today. What are *your* plans for the afternoon?

CLARENCE. Oh, I thought I'd go to our cabin and bone up on the specifics of Early Carib artifacts of the aboriginal indigenes. I wouldn't want to overlook one if it turned up in a native market.

ANGELICA. Clarence, I do wish you'd work up an interest in birds and bees that weren't petrified.

CLARENCE. Mother, there is more to life than sex.

ANGELICA. And there's more to a layer cake than sugar—but just try baking one without any!

(CLARENCE *laughs and exits, right*)

LORENZO. Your son, he is joking, yes?

ANGELICA. My son is an archaeologist. They don't know any jokes.

(*brightens as* DEBBY *enters, left*)

Ah, good afternoon, my dear!

DEBBY. Good afternoon, Mrs. Bostick. Isn't it a lovely day!

ANGELICA. Oh, let's skip the preliminary chitchat and get down to basics: Clarence is in our cabin, alone and unguarded.

DEBBY. Oh boy! . . . That is—thank you very much—well—if you'll excuse me—

LORENZO. Ah, but wait! May I not be introduced to this fair young flower?

ANGELICA. If she's *lucky* you may not be.

LORENZO. *Senorita,* I am Lorenzo La Jolla, your captain, who worships at your feet!

ANGELICA. You sure left *my* shrine in a hurry! All right, you win—this is Debby Tremayne.

LORENZO. (*bows to kiss* DEBBY'S *hand, then pauses*) Tremayne? Would you be—? But of course! I see the resemblance now! I have heard so much about you from your mother—on her last voyage with me—that is, with this ship.

DEBBY. Oh! You're the one who sent those flowers to—uh—Mom! She—was certainly surprised.

LORENZO. I cannot *wait* to see her again!

DEBBY. I'm afraid you're going to *have* to. She—wants nothing more to do with you. She told me.

LORENZO. Ha! She was always that way. A hundred times she would come to tell me she could never see me again. I am used to it. It means nothing.

DEBBY. But—uh—things have changed. *Mom* has changed. *Boy,* has she changed! You wouldn't even recognize her! So please—don't even try.

LORENZO. You are not making sense.

DEBBY. That's only because—uh—I'm in kind of a hurry. Excuse me! (*exits rapidly, right*)

LORENZO. (*eager to pursue her*) And now, if *you* will excuse *me*—?

ANGELICA. Hold the phone, Captain Hotblood! I should warn you, there is a large man named Tremayne who would dearly love a Latin nose to punch! So if you have designs on his wife or daughter—

LORENZO. Bah! Men of medicine never punch anybody. Their fingers are too important to their careers.

ANGELICA. He's a doctor? I didn't realize. I adore medical men! What's his specialty?

LORENZO. One that you would specially adore: He is a gynecologist.

ANGELICA. Oh, and I have symptoms I haven't even used yet! Lorenzo, you're a treasure! If there's one thing a woman enjoys even more than a hot romance, it's a discussion of her internal organs! And talk about luck—here he comes now!

(*She smiles winningly as* HARRY *enters, left, in slacks, blazer and yachting cap;* LORENZO *tries to tiptoe away.*)

HARRY. Hello, Mrs. Bostick! Beautiful day, isn't it? Well—

ANGELICA. Oh, surely you're not going to pass by without stopping to chat?

HARRY. I'd like to, but really, I'm meeting my wife in the lounge for cocktails. She's waiting there now.

(*At this,* LORENZO *stops his sneaky exit, straightens, adjusts his jacket, and is about to stride off, when:*)

ANGELICA. Why, Lorenzo, going so soon? I don't believe you two have met—?

HARRY. Lorenzo? Hey, are you the joker who sent those day-old flowers to my wife?

LORENZO. Which are you upset about—the flowers or their condition?

ANGELICA. (*to* HARRY) Oh, please don't rush off! Sit here beside me for a moment.

HARRY. But—I really should meet my wife—and besides, this guy here has something coming!

LORENZO. (*hastening his already-started exit*) Senor Tremayne, we will talk later, yes? (*bolts from sight*)

HARRY. (*trapped by* ANGELICA'S *invitation, shouts after him*) We will talk later, *hell* yes! (*sits uneasily on edge of chair beside hers*) Now, really, I mustn't dally too long—

ANGELICA. (*confidently*) But you will. You are a gentleman, and by that fact at the mercy of every lady who recognizes it. That's why ladies invented courtly etiquette. It makes men so easy to push around.

HARRY. Don't be so sure I'm well-mannered. I might just surprise you.

ANGELICA. Now-now, no hedging. You must be a perfectly charming man to have produced so charming a daughter.

HARRY. You mean—Debby? Debby's not my daughter.

ANGELICA. But—oh—I see. Your wife had a daughter when you married her?

HARRY. (*chuckles*) I rather doubt it. We were married right after high school. Hey, what's my wife got to do with Debby?

ANGELICA. She's Debby's mother. Debby said so. In fact, so did Lorenzo!

HARRY. (*gives very uneasy look in direction* LOREN-ZO *vanished*) That's crazy. You're being ridiculous.

ANGELICA. All I know is, Debby told Lorenzo her *Mom* didn't appreciate him sending those flowers, and Lorenzo told Debby he could see her resemblance to her— Oh. Oh my. Oh, what have I done! You—you didn't *know*!

HARRY. (*stands, aghast*) You're nuts! The whole notion is nuts! There's nothing *to* know!

ANGELICA. (*trying to pretend the situation weren't horrible*) Of course. I must have misunderstood them. Don't think about it at all, it's just a silly mistake, and you should put the whole thing right out of your mind . . . you poor man.

HARRY. You know—Debby *was* born while I was overseas in the Army . . .

ANGELICA. How *long* were you overseas?

HARRY. Only ten months . . .

(*Both react; then he suddenly shakes his head violently.*)

No! What am I thinking of! I'm sure there's a plausible explanation!

ANGELICA. Of course there is!

HARRY. It's really laughable!

ANGELICA. Hilarious.

HARRY. You just misunderstood them.

ANGELICA. I often do.

HARRY. Well—

ANGELICA. Well—

HARRY. (*with a forced smile matching her own*) Would you excuse me? My wife is expectant—*expecting* me! (HARRY *gallops frenziedly off, right*)

ANGELICA. (*calling after him*) I'll see you later. And please don't worry. You poor man.

(*Projection with deck chairs—and* ANGELICA *on hers— slides off, and backdrop-curtain rises, and we are in.*)


## ACT ONE, SCENE FIVE

*The ship's lounge. Three men sit at upstage bar, facing upstage, on swivel-type bar stools.* PEGGY, *in a crisp and glamorous cocktail dress, sits at one of two chairs at a small table just downstage of right center.* WAITER *approaches her from left, pauses at her side.*

WAITER. Are you sure you won't have something while you wait, Mrs. Tremayne?

PEGGY. Oh—perhaps I will, after all. My husband can always catch up with me when he arrives.

WAITER. Will you have your usual?

PEGGY. My usual what?

WAITER. Captain La Jolla has already told the bartender your preference in drinks.

PEGGY. How—how very kind of him. Uh—what *is* my preference, did he say?

WAITER. A "Yellow Bird"—very popular in the Caribbean—lime juice, curacao, rum, orange juice, and a whole banana.

PEGGY. Sounds just great for a Vitamin C deficiency. Okay, why not!

WAITER. (*moves to bar, calls off left*) One "Yellow Bird" for Mrs. Tremayne!

(*Each of three men will swivel toward her on his line.*)

MAN -1. Did you say "Mrs. Tremayne"?
MAN -2. "Mrs. *Margaret* Tremayne"?
MAN -3. "*The* Mrs. Margaret Tremayne"?

(PEGGY *reacts, and faces down front in terror, as each man jumps from his stool on his line:*)

MAN -1. Wow-dow!
MAN -2. I agree!
MAN -3. And she seems to be free!

(*Music starts, and they move down to encircle her, on:*)

TRIO. (*sings*)
Hey, Mrs. Tremayne! We'd like to mount a campaign
To join you swinging in the jet set,
And right away, so lady, get set!
Hey, Mrs. Tremayne! Don't turn us down with disdain!
We hear you're tops at effervescin',
So how's about a little lesson?

(PEGGY *reluctantly lets them draw her to her feet, and move her toward "dance area" between her table and the bar, though her face is toward us, and she is addressing us with her thoughts, on:*)

PEGGY. (*sings*)
I have a sad suspicion they presume I'm Madge!
What's worse, it's a tempting situation
To think that frisky frolics I am apt to cadge
Give me the fun and Madge the reputation!
  TRIO.
Hey, Mrs. Tremayne! You'll have no cause to
  complain
When far from us we make the blues wing,
While with your help we make this cruise swing
Out of sight!
Hey, Mrs. Tremayne! Let's live tonight!

(*Despite herself, she joins them in dance, at the finale of
      which, each man drops to one knee before her in
      turn, on his line.*)

MAN -1. Hey, Mrs. Tremayne!
MAN -2. Hey, Mrs. Tremayne!
MAN -3. Hey, Mrs. Tremayne!
TRIO. Let's live tonight!

(LORENZO *enters right;* TRIO *sees him, heads for bar.*)

MAN -1. Oops!
MAN -2. School's out!
MAN -3. We'll see you later, lady!

(*They re-perch as at top of scene;* PEGGY *hastens back
      to sit at her table, clumsily trying to hide her face
      from* LORENZO *with one hand, as if resting her
      cheek on that palm; but he is not one to be fooled.*)

LORENZO. Excuse me—it isn't—? No, it is not! You
are not the woman I thought you were—are you?
PEGGY. (*abruptly clutches his hand with both of hers*)
All right! I'm an imposter! But please—sir—Captain La
Jolla—may I—take you into my confidence?

LORENZO. (*likes what he sees, sits in vacant chair beside her*) Mrs. Tremayne—you may take me any place you choose!

PEGGY. Oh, that's wonderful! (*sees he is holding her hand*) I think.

LORENZO. Now, why do you pretend to be Mrs. Tremayne?

PEGGY. Oh, I don't. I am. But not the other one. She's my sister-in-law.

LORENZO. And you murdered her for her ticket?

PEGGY. (*laughs*) Really, it's very simple. My husband—that is, her husband—well, there was this convention—*is* this convention—but Debby's heart was set on—is *still* set on—Come to think of it—it's *not* very simple.

LORENZO. *Bueno*! I *like* long stories from lovely ladies! But first, one thing: This large man who threatens to punch my nose—he *is* or is *not* your husband? No, wait, it is not really important.

PEGGY. Well, it's *your nose*!

LORENZO. Ah, but I do not think a man of medicine would—Ah, but—if *you* are not—then *he* is not—yet, he must be *something*—?

PEGGY. (*very conscious that he still holds her hand*) Harry runs a flower shop. He's really very knowledge-able about it. And I love him very much.

LORENZO. Loyalty. I admire you for it. No—I *adore* you for it! (*takes her other hand as well, starts kissing both*)

PEGGY. Stop! People will see you! What will they think!

LORENZO. They will obviously think you are the *other* Mrs. Tremayne. If you must play the little game—I will help you pretend! (*tries for more kisses, but she pulls her hands away*)

PEGGY. No! I—I only did it because of Debby, but—if you're going to carry on this way—well—I'll explain to Harry somehow!

LORENZO. Aha! Your husband does not *know* you sail under a false name! *Bueno*! I shall *help* you to deceive him!

PEGGY. How do you mean that?

LORENZO. Why do you draw away? Do I not have the look of a man you can trust?

PEGGY. Yes. You do. You certainly do. That's *why* I don't trust you.

LORENZO. That does not make sense. Does it?

PEGGY. It's this way—if you're the kind of man I'm afraid you *might* be, the only way you could be a *success* at it is by not *looking* like the kind of man you are, so I can't be sure if you're what you *seem* to be, or just what you *want* to seem to be— (*abruptly laughs at herself*) And please don't ask me to repeat all that!

(*As a baffled* LORENZO *is about to do that very thing,*
　　PEGGY *sees* HARRY *entering lounge, and panically*
　　*urges:*)

My husband! Say nothing! *Por favor*?

LORENZO. (*stands as* HARRY *reaches table*) Senor Tremayne—I wish to say that I have made a grievous mistake. This is not the woman I thought she was. I apologize most deeply, dear lady, for sending those flowers.

PEGGY. Oh, don't! They *were* lovely!

LORENZO. You must prove you accept my apology by dining at my table tonight!

HARRY. Go ahead, Peg. *I* can always have a *sandwich* sent to the *room*!

PEGGY. Harry, you know very well he means you, too!

LORENZO. (*almost kisses her hand, senses* HARRY'S *look, shakes it instead*) Then—until tonight!

PEGGY. (*smiling dopily after* LORENZO *as he exits*) Till tonight—!

HARRY. (*sits beside her*) Jiggers, your husband is watching. (*she snaps from trance with a nervous laugh*) I'm certainly glad to hear him say you're the wrong *"hermosa Margarita"*! . . . You are, aren't you?

PEGGY. Honey, a woman *never* forgets a man who looks like Fernando Lamas! It's just—this trip and all—it's so—new—exciting—different—

HARRY. And don't forget "weird"! You wouldn't *believe* the conversation I just had with Angelica Bostick! (*looks up as* WAITER *arrives with* PEGGY'S *drink*) Say, that looks good. What is it?

WAITER. A "Yellow Bird," sir. The lady's favorite. Would you like the same?

HARRY. Uh—yeah, sure. Thanks. (as the WAITER *exits*) What did he mean "favorite"? Peg—you never had one of those things before, did you? No, don't even answer that. I'm being an idiot. Of course you didn't! Wonder what's in it?

PEGGY. Lime, curacao, rum, orange juice and a banana. (*sees his look*) I *suppose* . . . !

HARRY. Well, anyhow, you wouldn't believe the crazy story Angelica was telling me about why Debby was calling you "Mom"!

PEGGY. Oh, dear! What did she say?

HARRY. (*suddenly scared*) Why? What do you *think* she said?

PEGGY. (*pats his hand*) I'm sorry. I guess you had to learn the truth sooner or later. I was a fool to think I could keep it a secret forever!

HARRY. (*crushed, but kind*) How—how did it happen?

PEGGY. I hardly know. I mean, it happened so *fast*. One minute I was a contented housewife—the next I was embarking on a major deception! Silly, wasn't I!

HARRY. *Silly*?! Aren't you even a little *ashamed*?!

PEGGY. Oh—I was, at first—but then—after I thought it over—I figured it really wasn't such a bad idea after all!

HARRY. (*appalled*) Peg! This isn't like you!

PEGGY. (*thoughtfully*) It isn't, is it! I guess it's just that I'm starting to agree that Madge was right about the whole thing.

HARRY. *Madge* knows?!

PEGGY. Honey, it was Madge's *idea*!

HARRY. Good grief! I might have known!

PEGGY. Yes, I was pretty certain you'd figure out what I'd been *up* to when *Debby* came along!

HARRY. (*lurches to his feet*) How can you sit there and talk about it so calmly?!

PEGGY. Oh, Harry, what's done is done. I mean, here we are, and there's no turning back, right? Actually, I'm glad the truth finally came out. Now maybe you'll understand why I want you to keep your hat on.

HARRY. You mean keep my shirt on, don't you?! (*whirls, starts storming off in a pained daze*)

PEGGY. Harry? What are you so upset about? After all, honey, I did it for *your* sake!

HARRY. (*reels, turns to face her just short of exit*) *My* sake?

PEGGY. I thought it would give you a nice rest.

(HARRY *gives an incoherent cry, turns, and lurches out.*)

WAITER. (*arriving with drink*) What's happened to your husband?

PEGGY. Funny, I was just asking myself that very question!

(*Table area with* PEGGY *and* WAITER *slides off right,*

*bar with* TRIO *slides off left, and lounge-backdrop rises, and we find ourselves in:)*


## ACT ONE, SCENE SIX

*The ship's dining room. The Captain's table is just upstage of center, beneath a large chandelier. When our principals are finally seated,* LORENZO *will be at extreme left, with* ANGELICA *and then* PEGGY *on his right,* HARRY *at extreme right, and then* DEBBY *and* CLARENCE *on the downstage side on* HARRY'S *right. The deck will lie offstage right, and serve as entrance and exit for the principals;* WAITER *will make entrances and exits left. [NOTE: When the chandelier begins to sway, all will sway similarly; that is, keep their bodies from head-to-hips in a line parallel with the shaft of the chandelier; if desired, there can be a pair of portholes at upstage wall, one above* HARRY, *one above* LORENZO, *and horizon (dark sea and lighter night sky) visible through them, with sea and sky moving correspondingly with chandelier, to give total illusion of a very rough passage.] As scene begins,* HARRY—*dressed just as last seen—is alone at table with a full wine glass and almost-empty wine bottle; he is slightly sozzled. A moment after scene begins,* DEBBY—*in a lovely evening gown—will enter, stop at the sight of* HARRY, *then proceed to her place at the table. [Others will also be in elegant evening garb when they arrive.]*


DEBBY. Uncle Harry! Where have you been all afternoon? Aunt Peggy's been frantic!

HARRY. In our stateroom.

DEBBY. But she looked in the stateroom.

HARRY. When she looked in the stateroom, I was in the lounge. When she came to the lounge, I went back to the stateroom.

DEBBY. But why? Are you mad at her, or what?

HARRY. Not mad at, just baffled by. It's not so much what she's done, it's her attitude. Callous I could understand, but—*blasé*?

DEBBY. Well, what's done is done.

HARRY. That's fine from *your* point of view! (*looks at her, smiles sorrowfully*) You're so lovely. Just like your mother before you were born, years before she got married!

DEBBY. Did you know her then?

HARRY. I thought I did! (drains wine glass, refills it) Strangers when we meet—strangers when we part—you think you know a person—but no one knows anyone— not really—

DEBBY. Honestly, Uncle Harry, it's scary hearing you talk this way . . .

HARRY. I know. I get frightened every time I listen.

(PEGGY *enters on* CLARENCE'S *arm, and* ANGELICA *on* LORENZO'S; *All come to places at table, during:*)

PEGGY. Harry! Where in the world have you been?!

HARRY. Oh—here, there, the other place—it's a big boat. (*to* ANGELICA) Excuse me for not rising—I haven't forgotten my manners, but I can't seem to remember how to work my legs.

ANGELICA. I understand. It's all my fault, you poor man.

PEGGY. Nonsense! No matter what you told him, he shouldn't use that as an excuse to start draining every bottle in sight!

CLARENCE. (*conversationally*) The Carib Indians had no liquor at all in their culture before the Spanish came. They drank nothing but fruit juice, milk and water.

DEBBY. They must have thrown some pretty dull parties.

LORENZO. (*as* WAITER *approaches the table*) Ah, those fortunate natives! The wines of Spain are very difficult to resist.

HARRY. Who's resisting?

PEGGY. Harry! Honey, don't you think you'd feel better if you lay down?

HARRY. Probably. But that floor's pretty hard.

WAITER. Uh . . . shall I begin serving dinner, sir?

LORENZO. By all means! I think we will all feel better once that most elegant food begins to arrive!

(WAITER *will exit, and during remainder of scene will re-enter and exit regularly, with soup, salad, etc.*)

HARRY. Peg—maybe I misunderstood you this afternoon—don't you even feel a little bit contrite?

PEGGY. Well, of *course* I do! I took advantage of you, and I'm sorry.
<br>(*then, as he starts to brighten*)
But deep down, Harry—sincerely—aren't you kind of glad I did?

HARRY. (*slumps*) There she *goes* again! (*shakes head, takes large swallow of wine*)

PEGGY. Harry—honey—please stop drinking. Can't you at least be happy about what I did, for *Debby's* sake?

HARRY. (*this touches him*) Yeah—yeah, I can't argue that! Wouldn't swap her for anything. But, still and all, Peg— (*looks up as chandelier jingles and moves slightly*) What was that?

LORENZO. The sea is a bit rough tonight. But don't let that bother you. After all, this is a vacation—a fun trip—and our food and drink is the best in all the Caribbean—and most important of all—the captain's table gets the largest portions!

(*Others laugh, then look a bit apprehensive as waltz rhythm begins in orchestra, and smiles are strained slightly as song begins, in tempo with the gently swinging chandelier.*)

ANGELICA.
The chandelier sways as the boat hits a trough.
   HARRY.
We'd get on much better if we could get off.
   PEGGY.
The table's a-tilt and the soup leaves your bowl.
   CLARENCE.
The silverware fox-trots—
   DEBBY.
—as we rock and roll!
   ALL.
Dining's a joy at the captain's table!
Food's ready, he's willing, and we're nearly able
To eat, drink, be merry and come fill the cup!
   HARRY.
The captain can handle whatever comes up!
   CLARENCE.
I haven't the heart to pursue the soufflé .
   HARRY.
I can't hold my liquor: It's sliding away.
   LORENZO.
May I tell a joke?
   PEGGY.
I'm not fit for that game!
   ANGELICA.
The man enjoys gagging!

DEBBY.
I can't say the same!
ALL.
Dining's a joy at the captain's table!
Although things are spilling, and somewhat unstable,
Let's eat, drink, be merry and come fill the cup!
HARRY.
I'm suddenly sober and sick as a pup!

(*Tempo has been increasing, and the lovely chords are
beginning to turn fiendishly jarring, and the
group—excepting* LORENZO—*is starting to look
very ill, and to try to cling to the table-edge as they
continue.*)

PEGGY.
I knew you'd regret all the wine you just drank!
ANGELICA.
My spirits are sinking!
DEBBY.
My stomach just sank!
CLARENCE.
The bow plunges downward, as onward we forge!
Then, as the stern rises—
ALL.
Why, so does our gorge!
LORENZO. (*rises, holding glass as if for a toast*)
Dining's a joy at the captain's table!
Food's ready, I'm willing, and surely you're able
To eat, drink, be merry and refill each cup!
The gravy's delicious—!
ANGELICA. (*apalled at the mention*)
Lorenzo, shut up!
ALL. (*standing on wobbly legs, clinging to table-edge*)
We cannot remember why we felt such glee
Today when our ship left the port for the sea!
Our friends were all jealous, their envy was keen.

PEGGY.
So how come it's us who are turning bright green?!

(*By now, chandelier, sea-levels, waltz music, and body-lurchings are one step short of violent.*)

ALL.
Dinner is done at the captain's table!
Unsteady, unwilling, and no longer able
To say as we sway till we can't sip or sup—

(PEGGY *will continue clinging to table, while* HARRY, ANGELICA, DEBBY *and* CLARENCE *try to make it to the exit, in waltz-time* [1-2-3 forward—1-2-pause back], *each clapping a hand to mouth at appropriate moment:*)

HARRY.
The captain—*ulp!*
ANGELICA.
Captain can handle—*ulp!*
DEBBY.
Handle whatever—*ulp!*
CLARENCE.
Handle whatever comes—*ulp!*

(*Frantic underbeat starts as they lurch and stagger and reel backward and finally manage to exit, leaving* LORENZO *to complete the song in mystification.*)

LORENZO.
I give up!
(*Orchestra finishes with crashing chord; he turns to still-standing* PEGGY.)
Apparently you are made of sterner stuff than the others—
PEGGY. Only by about ten seconds! (*hand over mouth, lurches toward exit*)
LORENZO. Can I get you anything?

PEGGY. (*a swaying pause just short of exit*) Yes! *Dry land*! (*gallops offstage*)

WAITER. (*just arriving at table*) Mrs. Tremayne has not the good stomach for sailing you said she had.

LORENZO. It matters not. She will love tomorrow, when the ship docks at our first excursion-stop on Tumbango!

WAITER. Where the simpleminded tourists seek out stupid souvenirs.

LORENZO. Tumbango has color. That is what our guests pay for, color, at the charming native marketplaces.

WAITER. (*starting off*) They could get just as good a clipping at the ship's barbershop!

LORENZO. It is all part of the game. The tourists try to impress the natives, the natives try to impress the tourists, everybody lies and cheats everybody else—it is all—well—what you might call—

WAITER. (*pauses short of exit*) The Caribbean equivalent of a peace conference.

(LORENZO *reacts;* WAITER *exits; colorful tropic-forest-type backdrop descends, leaving about a four-foot area usable at extreme downstage, and we are in:*)


ACT ONE, SCENE SEVEN


*The native marketplace on Tumbango. Music starts as soon as backdrop has descended. Native* WOMAN *enters, singing to someone offstage.*


WOMAN.
Ship's in!
Time to look alive because soon this place will be

swarming
With rich, eager and tasteless *viajeros!*

(*Other natives, male and female, will appear from both
sides, some carrying baskets, some wheeling
wicker-type wheeled display stands; all their wares
are bright and colorful—the bead-feather-and-
seashell sort—and their costumes are no less
rainbow-hued; they will set up shop as they sing,
and be ready for business by the time our Principals
enter [dressed like tourists—sandals, flowered-
print shirts and dresses, cameras slung about necks,
etc.]*)

MAN.
And when they arrive they'll expect to see us smiling
And carefree and shouting for all their *dineros!*
WOMAN –2.
Do not begrudge what we have to give.
MAN –2.
No, but such a way we have to live—
ALL. (*spoken*)
Imitation primitive!
       (*then they sing harmoniously*)
*Melodia mercado!*
Put out your wares for all the world to see.
Tourists need a souvenir
To remind them they were here,
The while we sing our Market Melody.
*Melodia mercado!*
Though there are other things we'd rather do,
We must grin and smile and sing,
Sell a hat, a pot, a ring,
And make them think they got a bargain, too!
Make this one of their happiest days.
The happy tourist is the tourist who pays.

So charm these *viajeros* with our quaint native ways,
And whatever you do, don't speak too good the *Ingles*!

(PEGGY, HARRY, DEBBY, CLARENCE, ANGELICA *and*
    LORENZO *enter, strolling, examining the native
    wares*)

PRINCIPALS.
This odious *mercado,*
In which we'd not be normally caught dead,
Is the sort of market where,
If you haggle, they don't care,
'Cause any price they get, they're still ahead!
    CLARENCE.
May I see a rare authentic hand-tooled trinket?
    MAN.
Here is trinket, tooled as only native can.
    CLARENCE.
Yes, it's native, native as can be! I think it
Was made by an island native of Japan!
    HARRY.
*Melodia mercado*!
I'm so hung-over, my head's one big bruise!
    PEGGY.
All night, I said, "Come to bed!"
But you drank and drank, instead!
Now your nose must be the reddest on this cruise!
    HARRY.

        (*spoken, as he tries on fancy sunglasses*)
Please excuse!
    DEBBY.

    (*holding up necklaces to sunlight for inspection*)
*Melodia mercado*!
Is this the place where Clarence might succumb?
All this jew'lry I could buy—
Maybe catch his jaded eye—
If only he were not so very dumb!

PEGGY.
*Melodia mercado*!
Poor Harry, after oh-so-many years,
Looks like he's lost ev'ry friend—
  MAN -2.
Lady, how about you spend
Ten *pesos* to adorn your lovely ears?
  WOMAN. (*to* ANGELICA)
Would the lady like some real red-hot love-potion?
  ANGELICA.
Is it guaranteed to help me land a man?
  MAN.
It will give an even stubborn man strong notion!
  ANGELICA.
Do you have it in a twenty-four-ounce can?
  MARKETEERS.
*Melodia mercado*!
If they don't leave soon, we'll all go berserk!
Our commercial life we'd trade
To sit idly in the shade,
But, unhappily, to eat we have to work!
  PRINCIPALS.
      (*with souvenirs, start to re-gather to leave*)
Well, our primal marketplace is now behind us.
Surely we'll see dozens, but let's not keep score.
Prob'ly ev'ry marketplace will soon remind us
Of the one we all just saw the day before!
  MARKETEERS.
      (*in perfect barbershop harmony*)
The day before . . .
  ALL.
Let's sing it out with bravado!
As natives drum up business, who can frown?
Though the bargaining is crook-ed,
And the tourists end up rook-ed,
It's a joy to know you shook a drummer down.

So be an *aficionado*
Of stinking trinkets 'neath the tropic sun.
Native wares that get the nod owe
Quite a bit to the Mikado,
But a native desperado's so much fun!
    MARKETEERS. (*barbershopping again*)
We're so much fun!
    ANGELICA.
Though it's all the bunk,
Still our cash we'll plunk—
    CLARENCE/DEBBY.
Then we'll stash the junk
In our steamer trunk!
    HARRY.
And at home I'll say,
"Was I drunk that day?"
    PEGGY.
And I'll answer, "Yes, you were!"
    MARKETEERS.
(*The barbershop again, and getting a surprised reaction
    from* HARRY *and* PEGGY *at this intrusion into their
    affairs*)
You surely were . . . !
    ALL.
But don't lose your grip!
Keep one point in view:
When you take a trip
And the natives take you,
It's a pleasant bit of reciprocity!
    MARKETEERS. (*barbershop*)
Yes, sir! *Si-si!*
    ALL.
On *melodia mercado* we all agree!

(*On final sustained note, Principals exit one way, while
    Natives exit the other, with carts, baskets, etc., and
    as the last of them vanishes, backdrop rises on:*)

### Act One, Scene Eight

*The ship's pharmacy. Counter, shelves, white-jacketed*
PHARMACIST *behind counter.* DEBBY *and*
CLARENCE *enter, garbed as last seen, but minus*
*souvenirs, cameras, etc.*

PHARMACIST. Can I help you, Mister Bostick?

CLARENCE. What have you got for an upset stomach?

PHARMACIST. I think I have just the thing in the back
room—(*exits*)

DEBBY. You shouldn't have let your mother drink all
that love-potion.

CLARENCE. How could I stop her, punch her in the
eye?

DEBBY. You could have pointed out that she's supposed to have a *man* take the potion, not drink it
herself!

CLARENCE. It was ninety proof. She couldn't resist.
Now I suppose she'll fall for the first man she sees. Of
course, Mother *always* falls for the first man she sees.

DEBBY. You know—you're not the first man *I've* ever
seen—but other than that—I'm a *lot* like your mother.

CLARENCE. Debby, you can't *possibly* be crazy about
me. I give you absolutely no encouragement what-
soever.

DEBBY. Clarence, that's just the point! From the moment we met, you quite obviously couldn't stand me.
That means we're meant for each other! Don't you ever
go to the movies?

CLARENCE. Debby, this is real life. Sometimes love
*stays* one-sided!

DEBBY. Nonsense. Once one person feels love at first
sight, it's just a matter of time before the other person
feels it, too! Maybe you're not stuck on me—but you're
stuck in the story-line!

CLARENCE. Debby, use your head. Have I ever given you the slightest reason to like me?

DEBBY. Who says I *like* you?

CLARENCE. (*feels oddly discomfitted*) *Don't* you—?!

DEBBY. Oh, Clarence, honey, I can do a lot better than *that*!

(*sings*)

Me, I love you!
Me, I care!
Me, I want you!
So, prepare!
Just because you
Were born to
Wear pants,
You look askance
At girls who push romance,
But,
Me, I love you!
Me, I care!
Me, I want you!
So, beware!
Love lurks nearby!
It's here by design!
So, cold or hot,
Don't fight the plot!
Ready or not . . .
You're mine!

(*Throughout song she has been sidling around him, mussing his hair, etc., so that he is considerably less stand-offish than before when he speaks.*)

CLARENCE. Debby—you're impossible!

DEBBY. Not really. I'm just improbable! (*his reserve breaks, and he laughs*) There! I *am* getting to you! Help me prove I'm right! You tell me what I should wear to the big costume ball tonight, okay? What does a girl have to look like to ring an archaeologist's chimes?

CLARENCE. A Dead Sea Scroll.

DEBBY. Aw—!

CLARENCE. Well—wait—matter of fact—archaeologists *do* find attractions in *ancient* things, so—

DEBBY. I should dress as a grandmother?

CLARENCE. No-no! I mean—well, the Middle Easterners don't go in for harems the way they used to, but—I'll bet if they saw a harem girl they might think of reviving the custom.

DEBBY. (*pumps his hand*) Clarence, you've got a deal! And listen—there's a prize for the most original costume—if I win—what'll you give me?

CLARENCE. I'll buy you a eunuch.

DEBBY. No, *really*!

CLARENCE. Oh—look—first win the contest. Then—we'll see.

DEBBY. Now you're talking! Our romance is practically in the bag, Dad! . . . Get it? . . . "Baghdad"? See you at the dance, Ali Baba!

(*Laughs and exits, leaving* CLARENCE *teasingly holding his stomach in reaction to her dreadful line, as* PHARMACIST *re-enters behind him, holding spoonful of medication, on:*)

CLARENCE. My stomach can't take much more of this!

(*Turns, and* PHARMACIST *thrusts spoon into his mouth, leaving him standing stupefied with handle projecting, on:*)

PHARMACIST. That will be seventy-five cents.

(*Then both slide off with counter, and backdrop rises on:*)

## ACT ONE, SCENE NINE

*The deck outside archway leading to ship's ballroom. Passengers in paired costumes [Romeo and Juliet, Cleopatra and Antony, that sort of thing] enter from either side, laughing and chatting, and exit through archway left or right, behind it, to unseen ballroom. Posters flanking archway bear messages like "Costume Ball!" and "Prize for Most Original Costume!" with raked add-on strip across them saying "Tonight!" Amid moving throng,* HARRY *enters, wearing a tuxedo and a large white turban with jewel-and-plume above brow. As he nears archway,* LORENZO *enters, opposite, in full dress uniform.* HARRY *sees him and pauses. [NOTE: The **last** other-than-Principals masqueraders will exit at this time, and leave the area clear for plot-stuff.]*

HARRY. (*slightly smashed*) Hey, what a nifty costume! You look just like a sea captain!

LORENZO. (*politely*) Ship's personnel do not participate in the contest. What are *you* supposed to be—a rich man with a head-injury?

HARRY. (*laughs*) Hey, that's very good! No, I'm supposed to be an Arabian Pony-tate—Potenate—a rich Arab.

LORENZO. And your lovely *wife*?

HARRY. No, just a rich Arab.

LORENZO. (*impatiently*) I *mean*—what is *Mrs.* Tremayne coming as?

HARRY. As soon as possible!

(*Laughs, goes happily reeling into ballroom, with an irritated* LORENZO *following; then* CLARENCE, *in bright dashiki and tarboosh, enters, hesitates by ballroom entrance, looking about anxiously;*

ANGELICA *enters, opposite, in harem out-*
*fit—brocaded vest, gauzy pantaloons, curly-toed*
*slippers, pillbox-type jeweled hat, and ear-slung*
*gauzy veil, which she pulls down beneath her chin*
*when she sees her son.*)

ANGELICA. Why, Clarence! How nice! We go together!

CLARENCE. Mother! Whatever possessed you to come dressed like that?!

ANGELICA. It was Harry's idea. He thought it would suit me. What do you think?

CLARENCE. (*meaning the dire situation*) Beautiful! Just beautiful! (*starts into ballroom*) Excuse me, Mother, I think I'm going to need a drink!

(*As he vanishes,* DEBBY *enters, in harem outfit identical*
*to* ANGELICA'S, *even to the colors; she pulls down*
*her veil beneath her chin, smiling brightly as she*
*says:*)

DEBBY. Good evening, Mrs. Bostick—*Oh!* (*belatedly reacts to similarity of outfits*)

ANGELICA. And that's putting it mildly! Who conned *you* into see-through bloomers?

DEBBY. Clarence. He said it would suit me.

ANGELICA. Well, I guess we know how *we* rate with the men! Chattels! Slaveys! Just another pretty face on a hot little body!

DEBBY. I'm sure it's not so. Men have more respect for women than to— (*stops as* PEGGY *enters, in also-identical outfit*)

ANGELICA. You were saying?

PEGGY. (*has reacted, stopped, and now approaches uncertainly*) Maybe I misunderstood—is the prize for the *least* original costume?

ANGELICA. No, but maybe there's a booby prize for women who listen to men! Who pulled the veil over *your* eyes?

PEGGY. Lorenzo. He said—

DEBBY/ANGELICA. —it suited you?

PEGGY. Oh, and I was so looking forward to the masquerade! But we can't go in like this?!

ANGELICA. Why not? We could go as a single entry: Three Generations of Servitude! . . . .*Men!*

DEBBY. *Men!*

PEGGY. *Men!*

    (*an exotic Arabian arpeggio sounds, and:*)

TRIO. (*sing*)

Men are no damn good! Men are no damn good!
The truth may hurt, but it's a certainty!
Any woman who says it isn't true
Has told a lie or needs psychiatry!

PEGGY.
Cook and scrub and dust and sew till you're too dead
To feel!

ANGELICA.
Then for your reward he takes you to his bed!

TRIO.
Big deal!
Any girls who would trade their maidenhood
For chains are girls with brains of solid wood!
Take a tip and throw out the mistletoe,
'Cause men are no damn good!

    (*they do a unified pseudo-Arabian shimmy; then:*)

DEBBY.
Men are for the birds! Ladies, mark my words!
They start as chums, but soon here comes the bride!

ANGELICA.
Then the dream goes bust, as you learn he's just
A valentine with Frankenstein inside!

PEGGY.
During courtship, though you found his gruff appeal
Ideal—
DEBBY/ANGELICA.
Afterwards, you find you're married to a real
Schlemiel!
DEBBY.
You're his loyalty, on the fam'ly tree—
ANGELICA.
But in-between, he seeks out greener wood!
PEGGY.
Where true love should flow—
DEBBY.
He's the undertow!
TRIO.
Oh, men are no damn good!

(*They shimmy again, then pause, and music continues
vamp [via percussion alone] as* HARRY, LORENZO
*and* CLARENCE *appear in archway for:*)

HARRY. Oh, *there* you are!
CLARENCE. My, you look nice!
LORENZO. Come along, the party's starting!
WOMEN. Right away!

(*Men exit into ballroom again, Women look at one
another, then pick up where they left off:*)

TRIO.
Men are immature! This we know for sure!
If they don't get their way, they sit and pout!
We should leave them flat, but if we did that,
What would there be for us to gripe about?
PEGGY.
For a lifestyle, only fools would let romance
Suffice!

DEBBY.
We should tell them off—
ANGELICA.
But when we get the chance—
TRIO.
No dice!
DEBBY.
Men have got us beat!
ANGELICA.
They're so stinking sweet!
PEGGY.
Though why they're fun we've never understood!
ANGELICA.
Yet, we never go!
DEBBY.
For, it's our fate to know—
PEGGY.
That we adore them so—
TRIO.
Though knowing, to our woe,
That men . . . are . . . no . . . damn . . . goooooooood!

(*They shimmy again, sustaining final note, then end with a sort of boom-boom hip-swing left and right on final two notes of melody*)

ANGELICA. Well, let's make the most of it, ladies. Face it, men will never change!

PEGGY. (*starting off the way she entered*) Maybe *they* won't, but *I'm* sure going to! (*exits*)

DEBBY. (*hesitating at ballroom entrance*) Do you think *we* should go in, dressed this way? Maybe we ought to change into something else.

ANGELICA. Listen, if I go back to my stateroom, I'm going to bed! Come on— (*links arms with* DEBBY) Let's enter the contest as a *Doublemint* commercial!

(*They start through archway, arm in arm, and as they do so, archway-wall and masking-wall behind it rise up out of sight, and they—and we—are now in:*)

ACT ONE, SCENE TEN

*The ballroom.* DEBBY *and* ANGELICA, *continuing their upstage movement from previous scene, join* HARRY, CLARENCE *and* LORENZO, *amid a chatting, happy group of costumed Passengers. The atmosphere is bright and alive, and the* WAITER *moves about with a tray of glasses of champagne, and band [i.e.: the pit orchestra] is softly playing "Me, I Love You" beneath dialogue.*

LORENZO. Ah, the ladies! But where is the charming Mrs. Tremayne?

ANGELICA. Oh, she'll be here, she'll be here. Now, which one of you gentlemen can I browbeat into asking me to dance?

HARRY. (*with a courtly—if unsteady—bow*) It would be my pleasure, dear lady. (*they dance away*)

DEBBY. Clarence—?

CLARENCE. Well—

LORENZO. He who hesitates is lost!
(*sweeps* DEBBY *away from* CLARENCE *onto dance floor*)

CLARENCE. (*watching them ruefully*) I should feel relieved. I wonder why I don't? (*takes glass of champagne from Waiter's tray, sips at it mournfully*)

ANGELICA. (*As she and* HARRY *dance to downstage left*) It's so marvelous to have you all to myself at last! Now I can get some free professional advice!

HARRY. Are you serious? I can't imagine a woman like you needing *my* assistance!

ANGELICA. I know why you're putting me off. You professional men hate to be approached outside office hours.

HARRY. No-no, really. I don't mind. What seems to be the problem?

(*Music will stop, and* HARRY *and* ANGELICA *will get champagne from passing waiter, and sip as they chat*)

ANGELICA. It's quite delicate. I guess you—you might say—the bloom is off the rose . . . I suppose it's inevitable—!

HARRY. Nothing inevitable about it. Not if you have the right equipment and know how to use it!

ANGELICA. (*not certain if she should feel insulted*) What do you mean—equipment?

HARRY. Well, the most *important* thing is, of course, your *spade*!

ANGELICA. (*chokes on champagne*) I'm *what*?

HARRY. (*busily slapping her on the back, misses her erroneous interpretation of his line*) Is that better?

ANGELICA. I'm not sure . . .

HARRY. Of course, I can't really make a competent diagnosis until I've made a thorough examination. How are your stems?

ANGELICA. Uh—well—I—haven't had any complaints! Did—uh—did you wish to come to my cabin to make that—examination—?

HARRY. Oh, is that where it's at?

ANGELICA. You have such a colorful way of phrasing things . . . I guess, why—yes! Why not! That's where it's *at,* all right!

HARRY. Was it very hard to get potted?

ANGELICA. I beg your pardon?

HARRY. I mean, I presume it was difficult to get out of your bed. In cases like yours, it usually is.

ANGELICA. How dare you!

HARRY. How dare I what?

ANGELICA. What you just said!

HARRY. But it's true! After all, when you take a cultured flower into a foreign environment, it may fail to reach full blossom without help.

ANGELICA. (*flattered by that "cultured flower"*) It's kind of you to offer me your—help . . .

HARRY. I don't anticipate much trouble.

ANGELICA. (*icing over*) Now, just a moment—!

HARRY. A little propping up here, a careful pinch here and there—

ANGELICA. Really! I draw the line at pinching!

HARRY. Oh, but pinching is very important if you want to start any little sprouts!

ANGELICA. What?!

HARRY. I suppose you're troubled by parasites, too? That can cause all sorts of premature wrinkling.

ANGELICA. Look here, buster—!

HARRY. If you'd like, I could spray for mildew, too. But only after the pinching. It gets lively faster, that way.

ANGELICA. (*very uneasy now, backing off*) Yes, yes, I'm sure it does. But—perhaps some other time—?

(LORENZO, *from across ballroom, starts toward them*)

HARRY. Oh, I wouldn't wait too long, if I were you. In this humid tropical environment, if you hold off the pinching too long, you could end up with a really bad case of crotch rot!

ANGELICA. (*in shock, lurches into* LORENZO'S *arms*) Captain! Take me away from this maniac!

(*starts off with him, as* HARRY *stares in bewilderment*)

You wouldn't believe the things he said! All he talks is dirt! Nothing but dirt!

LORENZO. What did you expect? After all, the man's an expert on dirt.

ANGELICA. You can say that again!

(*Then everyone looks up as* PEGGY *enters the ballroom, in a lavish gown, with flowers in her hair; she is easily the most beautiful sight in the Caribbean*)

LORENZO. (*abandoning* ANGELICA *and moving toward her*) I would not have believed one woman could have so much beauty!

PEGGY. You are very kind, Lorenzo.

LORENZO. But—this is a costume ball.

PEGGY. And this is a costume.

LORENZO. What are you supposed to be?

PEGGY. Can't you tell? I'm the belle of the ball!

LORENZO. (*takes her into his arms*) Indeed, that is what you are!

HARRY. Just a minute! That's my wife! Get your hands off her!

LORENZO. I was *only* about to *dance* with her!

HARRY. Not if you don't want your nose to win first prize as a pancake!

PEGGY. Harry, please, you're making a scene!

HARRY. You ain't seen nothing yet! You said this vacation would be relaxing and amusing! Well—I'm not relaxing—and I am not amused!

LORENZO. *Por favor, Senor* Tremayne—

HARRY. And I've had just about enough of *you,* Fernando!

LORENZO. *Who?*

PEGGY. (*stands tall, speaks tautly*) Harry, I don't know what's stuck in your craw, but I wish you'd spit it out!

HARRY. All right! It's you! Look at you! Belle of the ball! Ha! A woman your age—!

PEGGY. (*with icy control*) Keep it up, Harry, keep it up . . .

HARRY. If you could just *see* yourself—!

PEGGY. (*with growing rage*) I suppose you'd like me better in a housecoat and slippers, with egg on my hands and flour on my nose?! But Harry, that's precisely the way I'm *sick* and *tired* of seeing myself!

HARRY. I didn't mean—

PEGGY. And what *about* my age?! If I don't break out a little bit *now,* when *do* I break out?!

HARRY. Break out all you like! Just don't come crying to *me* for the *calamine* lotion!

PEGGY. (*stung, almost flares, but then subsides into an even more angry iciness, on:*) I won't. You can count on it. Because—Harry—I've got news for you. I am having a ball, for the first time in a long time, and no one is going to take this moment away from me! No one! So, whether you like it or not—
(*Music has been softly coming up in a rhythmic, angry under-melody, and as it reaches its peak, she sings:*)
Don't rock my boat! Don't despise a new horizon!
While romantic circumstance emancipates my foolish
    fancy,
If you're gonna jeer about it, I'm not gonna care!
Go ahead and sneer about it, I won't turn a hair!
For, when you're forty or more, if you don't know the
    score
By then and get under way, you won't go into extended
    play!
Let my boat float! Why destroy a joyous voyage?
Don't you scuttle my adventure!
If you're seeking penitence, you're
Riding for a fall! I will have a ball and never
Hear a word at all, though you caterwaul forever!

Now is the time to show how life's sublime and a wow,
      because
My ship's coming in, and happiness is waiting there on
      the bow!

(*Music soars, and* PEGGY *whirls from man to man, as
      all—excepting* HARRY, *who is sidelined at
      downstage left—get caught up in the excitement and
      sing:*)

      ALL.
Don't rock her boat!
      PEGGY.
Ah-aaaaah!
      ALL.
Don't tell her life's not worth living!
Don't say too much water's freely flowed across the dam,
When she's departing for romantic places!
      PEGGY.
Kicking over all the traces!
      ALL.
Laughing into all our faces!
      PEGGY.
Touching all the golden bases!
      ALL.
She is determined to be wild, abandoned and free to live
      life
Right at the top! You'll have to shoot her to get her to
      stop!
      ALL/PEGGY.
Let that boat float!
      PEGGY.
Ah-aaaaah!
      ALL.
Let it sail toward new horizons!
You may never beat the blahs,
But take us with you to the Casbah!

Isn't it enthralling that we're gonna have a ball!
Riding maybe for a fall and toward an overhaul!
Though we head into a squall and we may start to
   sprawl,
We have not the time to stall, 'cause, face it, after all:
Now is the time to show how life's sublime and a wow,
Because that ship has come in, and
Happiness is waiting there on the bow!

(PEGGY *whirls and dances with man after man, with
    wild abandon, as* HARRY *turns sorrowfully and
    starts off, as—*)


## THE CURTAIN FALLS


End of Act One

Act Two, Scene One

*The Tremayne stateroom, night.* PEGGY *is alone at the desk, in an attractive peignoir, mechanically twirling a party hat on one finger, looking pretty much ready to cry. Champagne waits in an ice bucket beside the desk, as does another party hat upon the desk, and a pair of stemmed goblets. The wall phone rings. She brightens instantly, runs to answer it.*

PEGGY. *Hello*? . . . Oh, hi, Debby. I—I thought you might be Harry . . . No, I haven't, not for hours, not since the dance . . . Where are you—? . . . That sounds like fun. How did you talk Clarence into a moonlight swim? . . . Oh, Debby, you *didn't*! With all his *clothes* on?! . . . Well, you're lucky he *could* swim! . . . He can't? Then how—? . . . Oh, that's not very good for *your* clothing, either! . . . Me? Oh—just passing the time away . . . I thought maybe I'd drop a line to your mother and tell her how things are going . . . No, not *everything*! . . . Oh, you know how vacation-letters go—a little of what's happening, and a lot of what you *wish* were happening . . . I'll think of something—even if I have to invent some of it . . . Okay, sweetheart, you'd better hurry back to him before he comes to. It's a shame he wasn't conscious enough to *appreciate* mouth-to-mouth resuscitation . . . Right. 'Bye now! (*hangs up, returns unhappily to stare at bottle; abruptly picks it up, uncorks it, and starts to pour a drink for herself, all this action while musing aloud:*) How *could* I approach a letter to Madge? . . . Tell all? Make

65

everything up? I suppose I could skip the sensitive topics—but that wouldn't leave me anything to write about except the weather. "The sun is shining. Whoopee!" Madge already *knows* that. That's what trips to the Caribbean are *for*! (*sits at desk, takes sip of champagne*) Mmm, that's good . . . now, let's see— What could I possibly say—?

(*Music starts softly; she ponders, then sings:*)
Dear Madge: You won't believe the life I'm leading,
Games I'm playing, cares I'm dumping,
Fun I'm having, drums I'm thumping,
Men I have misled!
Oh, Madge! I've been pulled over twice for speeding,
But when the policeman saw me,
He did not lay down the law, he
Stole a kiss instead!
(*The musingly slow tempo picks up as she elaborates.*)
Is it a lark? I hope to tell ya, kiddo!
And while I'm looking out for Number One,
My Harry's being chased by this rich widow,
And Debby's set her sights upon her son!
(*Tempo remains brisk as she returns to main melody.*)
So, Madge, this voyage sure is superseding
Keeping house and budget-watching!
I'm too busy cucaraching
While the chance endures!
I've gone beyond the Turkey Trot,
And made a name that's not so hot,
But luckily, the name I've got
Is yours!
(*Music continues, and backdrop from Tumbango Mar-*
*ketplace masks stateroom from view, even as she*
*muses aloud.*)
Let me see—what else could I tell her—?

[*NOTE:* PEGGY *is slipping out of peignoir, back of*
*drop, under which she wears tennis outfit, as we go*
*to:*]

### ACT TWO, SCENE TWO

*Backdrop represents your Basic Caribbean setting, no specific locale, and* PEGGY *[with the help of a microphone held by some helpful soul as she gets ready for her new entrance into this "daydream sequence"] can still be heard:*

PEGGY. (*over mike*)
Gee, Madge, I plunge along unchecked, unheeding,
Taking good advice from no one,
Join a party, or I throw one,
Till the stars unglue!
Then, Madge, to new excitement I'm proceeding!
While your Debby's seeking true love,
Or my husband's with his new love,
I find things to do . . .

(PEGGY *and trio of men from bar-scene in Act One, Scene Five, all four toting tennis rackets, dance on before drop, blithe and energetic, singing*)

TRIO.
Hey, Mrs. Tremayne!
PEGGY. (*spoken*) That's me!
TRIO.
Your tennis drives us insane!
PEGGY. (*spoken*) Aw, gee!
TRIO.
You don't know how to play the sport, yet
You've got the best form on the court, yet!
Hey, Mrs. Tremayne!
You show no strain and no pain!
How great your pep and ener-gee are!
It's great to know that you and we are
Hand-in-glove!
Hey, Mrs. Tremayne! The score is love!

(*As they complete dance-cross,* HARRY *and* ANGELICA
  *pass them as they enter, arm-in-arm, singing*)

HARRY.
My wife is away, and I'm happy to say
You're a lovable playmate to pinch!
ANGELICA.
I see by your smile you'd be fun to beguile!
If you won't take a mile, take an inch!
HARRY.
You mean you'd allow me to start here and now
With a regular powerhouse play?
ANGELICA.
To my arms you must fly for the time of your life, for—
BOTH.
My/your wearisome wife is away!

(*As they exit,* PEGGY *and* LORENZO *enter where* PEGGY
  *just exited—he is in uniform, she wears a comb and
  mantilla and flare-skirted Spanish dress; they are
  doing a merengue.*)

PEGGY.
Dancing with the captain,
Two strong arms I'm wrapped in!
I get really zapped in
Arms I can get trapped in!
Though he's very apt in
Time to use brute force,
When I'm with the captain,
He can plot the course!

(*Trio enters, and joins them in a dance that carries them
  off at finish, just as* CLARENCE *and* DEBBY *stroll
  on, at opposite side, hand-in-hand and cheek-to-
  cheek*)

CLARENCE.
I'm yours, all yours! As long as life endures!

DEBBY.
You're mine, all mine! There's bubbles in my wine!
    BOTH.
We're ours, and we shout without discretion:
It's great to be possessed by one's possession!
    CLARENCE.
I'm hers, all hers! My heart within me purrs!
    DEBBY.
I'm his, all his! My soul is full of fizz!
    BOTH.
Indoors or out, on train or bus,
Love can't go wrong since we belong to us. . . . !

(*They remain onstage as musical tempo picks up, and*
    PEGGY—*now in something fringed, spangled and*
    *golden—comes whirling on, followed by* LOREN-
    ZO, ANGELICA, HARRY, TRIO, STEWARD, *Waiter,*
    OFFICER, *Marketeers and assorted Passengers, all*
    *forming an adoring backdrop as she does the*
    *Marilyn-Miller pirouette-cross, and will finally exit*
    *offstage while they remain there to sing:*)

    ALL.
Don't rock her boat!
Don't encumber her big number!
Don't insist she's misbehaving!
Let her satisfy her craving!
Let her pull out all the stops
And dance the night away!
Let her dance until she drops!
Let Peggy have her day!
For, she's the one we adore!
And her shimmering choreography is a dream,
And all that we can do is just scream:
Encore!

*(Music builds, and all dance offstage, and then that Caribbean backdrop rises as music slows, and we are in)*

### ACT TWO, SCENE THREE

*The Tremayne stateroom.* PEGGY *is seated at desk, in peignoir again [NOTE: The preceding Spanish outfit and gold-fringe outfit are Velcro-fastened costumes that can go on instantly over the tennis outfit when she's offstage, for those fast changes.]; one cheek rests upon her fist, that elbow on the desktop, while other hand vainly tilts a now-empty champagne bottle over her half-filled goblet.*

PEGGY.
     *(sings wearily as she sets down bottle)*
Well, Madge, the moon is fading and receding,
Time I guess to put the lid on
Telling you the things I did on
This exciting cruise.
It's all been very grand and new,
And Madge, I owe it all to you.
Tomorrow's plans are certain to
Amuse . . . !

*(Her voice—and music—trail off; abruptly, she buries her face in her hands and sobs; there is a knock at the door; she hastily brushes tears away, jumps up and rushes to door, smiling hopefully;* ANGELICA *enters.)*

PEGGY. Oh . . . it's only you, Mrs. Bostick.
ANGELICA. I'm sorry to barge in so late. I—I believe I owe your husband an apology.

PEGGY. (*icily*) What did you do, fight him off?

ANGELICA. Peggy! Surely you don't imagine that Harry and I—?

PEGGY. (*nearer Sherlock Holmes than Clarence Darrow*) Oh, but surely I do! You talk of nothing but men. Harry is a man. He is not here where he belongs. Therefore, ergo, and also, *thus*—!

ANGELICA. Peggy, all Harry and I talked about were my female-troubles.

PEGGY. (*almost sobered by the thought*) *What*?!

ANGELICA. I know, I know. Lorenzo finally straightened me out about what Harry *really* does for a living. The poor man, I nearly slapped his face!

PEGGY. (*still a bit fuzzy*) Lorenzo's?

ANGELICA. No, your husband's. I mean, after all, when he talked about my *limbs* and my *trunk,* I thought he meant *my* limbs and *my* trunk!

PEGGY. (*starts a laugh, but stops it in puzzlement*) But— you *must* have known what Harry does—I mean, if you didn't know he was here as an imposter, how could you have blabbed to him about Madge and the tickets?

ANGELICA. Who is Madge? What tickets?

PEGGY. (*fingertips to temples*) I must be on the wrong wavelength—! Look—Harry came to me, shortly after we sailed, and said he'd found out the *truth* from *you*! I assumed he meant about Madge and the tickets.

ANGELICA. Oh, that! No-no, that has nothing to do with this Madge, whoever *she* is. I accidentally betrayed the fact that *you* are Debby's *mother*!

PEGGY. (*staggered*) *What*?! Where did you get a crazy notion like that?!

ANGELICA. Why, from Debby, of course . . . ?

PEGGY. Oh! Yes, but that was only because—! Oh, damn! If Harry had only said—but *I* thought he meant—and he thought *I* meant— (*the full horror strikes her*) And I nearly said we owed it all to his *brother*! (*clutches* ANGELICA *by one arm*) *Harry* won't even let his *brother* borrow his *lawnmower*!

ANGELICA. You mean—you're not—Debby isn't—? Oh, my stars, what have I done! Now I *really* owe him an apology!

PEGGY. And so do I! No wonder he got so uptight about Lorenzo! It's all beginning to make sense!

ANGELICA. *Ghastly* sense! (*starts for door*) I believe I'll delay my apology till you get yours over with. *I* was merely *insulted* on the *dance* floor. *You're* lucky you weren't *shot*! (*pauses in open doorway*) By the way, you don't know where I might find Clarence—?

PEGGY. I'm sorry to say, the last I heard, Debby had just pushed him into the ship's pool.

ANGELICA. Good for her. Clarence needs a push. He always pretends to himself that I need him so much he can never marry—at least, that's his excuse when romance lurks too near. What I really need are grandchildren!

PEGGY. Then you're not upset about her pushing him into the pool?

ANGELICA. Ha! His approach to romance is all wet, anyhow!

        (*Looks up as* HARRY *approaches*)
Ah, just the man I'm longing to see! However—someone else has a greater priority. Excuse me.

        (*As* HARRY *enters, she exits and shuts door*)

PEGGY. (*rushes toward him*) Harry! Oh, my sweet darling—! (*stops short as she sees the look on his face*)

HARRY. (*quietly*) Hello, Peg. I just had a long talk with Debby.

PEGGY. Debby? Isn't she with Clarence at the ship's pool?

HARRY. Not any more. They're off looking for towels and hot coffee. But never mind that. Peg—Debby explained everything. See, I thought—

PEGGY. Darling, I know what you thought, and it's all right. It's my fault, this whole silly mess.

HARRY. Wait, I'm not finished. I apologize for what I thought. I'm sorry to have doubted you for a moment. But—I'm past being sorry for what I felt when you walked out on me at that dance tonight. Oh, not physically—but you walked out on me as surely as if you'd slammed a door in my face. Breaking out, you said. Don't rock your boat. Okay. That's what you want—that's what you've got. I've talked with the purser—there are extra accommodations on board. I've taken them. Goodbye, Peg.

(*He exits quietly and shuts door;* PEGGY *stands stunned, then takes a step doorward, then stops; after a moment, she sits down, dazed, on chair, and:*)

PEGGY. (*sings quietly*)
Little fool, thought you played it smart.
Little fool, gambled with your heart.
You learned a lesson you don't learn in school, little
  fool.
Little fool, thought you knew each trick.
Little fool, but he caught on quick.
And dropped you like a penny in a pool, little fool,
  little fool.
Life held you fast and charmed you with its smile,
It sure fooled you for awhile. Who's to blame?
But that's all past, and now you're on the shelf,
Feeling sorry for yourself. What a shame!
Little fool, thought your fling would last.
Little fool, learned the hard way, fast.
Go find that dunce cap, and sit on your stool . . .
Little fool. Little fool.
(*Phone rings; she does not react till phone rings again; she rises listlessly and answers it*)
Hello—? . . . Oh, hello, Lorenzo . . . But—it's nearly

midnight! . . . Now, really, what would people think if I were to—to— (*stops, looks toward closed door, and then straightens, no longer listless, with fire in her eyes*) No. Wait. Come to think of it—that might be fun—the very thing I need right now! I've never been on a ship's bridge—alone—at midnight—with a Spaniard! . . . Sure! Why not! . . . I'll see you there in fifteen minutes! (*Hangs up phone, wipes final tear from her eyes with an angry sniff, and begins to undo the bow at the neck of her peignoir.*)

(*Promenade Backdrop from Act One, Scene Four descends and blocks her from view, and we are in:*)

### Act Two, Scene Four

*The Promenade deck.* CLARENCE *and* DEBBY *enter, both in soggy clothing, hair mussed and drizzling water down their faces. They wear large terrycloth robes cloak-fashion about their shoulders, and he is shivering.*

CLARENCE. Of all the dumb stunts! My best travel-knit suit! If the water didn't ruin it, I'm sure the chlorine will!

DEBBY. I was only trying to save your life.

CLARENCE. By pushing me into the pool?!

DEBBY. Well—you wouldn't stick around and talk—and if we don't talk, you won't get to know me—and you have to know me better before you can propose—and if you don't propose to me, you'll never marry me, and your life will be ruined! So—I saved you.

CLARENCE. If *you* think that *I* would *marry* you, *now*—!

DEBBY. Of *course* not now—it's the middle of the night!

CLARENCE. I mean *at all*!

DEBBY. Well, you gotta admit—I sure got you *talking* to me!

CLARENCE. Now, *listen*—!

DEBBY. (*adoringly*) *I'm* listening . . . ?!

CLARENCE. Oh, what's the use! It's a waste of time trying to reason with a mental case!

DEBBY. Oh, good, you're starting to feel sorry for me! First pity—then love!

CLARENCE. Get this straight: I'm feeling sorry for *me*! And the first thing isn't going to be pity—it's going to be pneumonia! (*sneezes noisily*)

DEBBY. What you need is a good stiff slug of brandy. Uh—I have a bottle in my stateroom.

CLARENCE. Much as that tempts me—since we couldn't find any hot coffee—if my mother found out I went to a young girl's room this time of night—!

DEBBY. Oh, come off it! You're no more a mama's-boy than *I* am! You just use your mother as an escape-clause when things get sticky!

CLARENCE. That . . . is . . . a . . . *lou*-sy thing to say! I happen to love and respect my mother. If she knew I was cavorting around with you, the shock might—it might—well, there's no telling what it might do!

DEBBY. Yeah, she'd be so stunned, it'd be at least ten seconds before she started sending out wedding invitations!

CLARENCE. Nonsense. Mother—wouldn't want me to marry beneath my station!

DEBBY. Clarence, you *couldn't* marry beneath your station. Nothing's lower than an archaeologist!

CLARENCE. And what's so bad about studying primitive cultures?

DEBBY. Nothing, if you *learn* from your studies! Clarence, honey, on a night like this, with a moon like that, and you a man, and me a woman—I'll bet your average primitive would have better things to do than discuss fossil-hunts!

CLARENCE. Debby, you've missed the *point*!

DEBBY. No, I *like* the top of your head! Now, come on, marry me!

CLARENCE. What, pointed head and all? Our children would all be idiots! Especially yours!

DEBBY. Oh, come down off your high-horse and enjoy yourself! I won't bite you—at least, not without a specific invitation!

(*sings*)

If you'd ask me for a dance, I would consent.
You'd find it an experience well spent.
Let's not waste all this lovely atmo*sphere* and sit!

CLARENCE.
Oh, no! Mother wouldn't hear of it!

DEBBY.
We could slip off to my cabin for a drink,
But if you're worried what your mom might think,
I'll do my best to overcome your fear of it!

CLARENCE.
Oh, no! Mother wouldn't hear of it!

DEBBY.
All that counts is, we're together!
Throw off your mother's tether and let's play!

CLARENCE.
Your brain's too much like a feather.
You're much too dumb for Mother, anyway!

DEBBY.
We could take a promenade about the deck,
And find a cozy spot where we could neck.
It's primitive, and might help your career a bit.

CLARENCE.
Oh, no! Mother wouldn't hear of it!
DEBBY.
Well, she wouldn't hear of it from me!
CLARENCE.
That's not what I meant!
DEBBY.
Come on, relent!
CLARENCE.
Well, I don't know—
DEBBY.
Come on, let's go!
CLARENCE.
But Mom might think—
DEBBY.
You need that drink!
CLARENCE.
I should refuse—
DEBBY.
But, oh, that booze!
CLARENCE.
I'd worry
If Mother ever heard of it—
DEBBY.
Let's hurry,
I'll never breathe a word of it!
CLARENCE.
It's indiscreet!
DEBBY.
But what a treat!
CLARENCE.
Oh, hell, let's go!
DEBBY.
And so there's no more fuss—
BOTH.
Mother wouldn't hear of it—
From us!

*(They hurry off arm-in-arm, laughing happily, and backdrop moves upward, and we are now in:)*


### ACT TWO, SCENE FIVE

*A double location: The ship's bridge, right, and* DEBBY'S *stateroom, left. The bridge is lighted, but the stateroom is at the moment dark.* LORENZO *and* PEGGY *enter the bridge; she was never so gorgeously gowned, nor he so Spanishly gallant. He shuts the door; she looks at it, then opens it.*

LORENZO. You do not feel safe with me. That is good.

PEGGY. I just didn't think we'd be this much alone. Shouldn't there be a helmsman at the wheel or something?

LORENZO. He has gone below. The ship is on the automatic pilot. Nothing can go wrong.

PEGGY. How do you mean that?

LORENZO. Any way you choose to take it.

    *(Starts to embrace her; she recoils.)*

PEGGY. No-no, you mustn't!

LORENZO. Yes-yes, I must!

PEGGY. Lorenzo, you just don't understand!

    *(A Tango intros, and she sings:)*

I really should not be here!
My footsteps went astray!
I don't know what came over me
To hurry here this way!
It must have been the moonlight
Combined with the champagne—
Or else the Caribbean
Causes water on the brain!

LORENZO.
>           (*With all his Latin-lover-stops pulled out.*)
> *Querida mia*! O, *por favor*,
> Don't be a snob,
> Let go the knob
> And shut the door!
>           (*pushes it closed*)
> This is the moment for sweet romance!
> Do not forswear it,
> Grin and bear it,
> Take a chance!

(*Sweeps her into the tango-rhythm, and they dance;
    meanwhile, CLARENCE and DEBBY enter her cabin,
    she turns on the lights, and—as CLARENCE, his
    back to her, looks about the room nervously—she
    shuts the door, produces a padlock, and uses it to
    fasten the door immovably shut, as he sings:*)

CLARENCE.
> I really should not be here!
> We're much too much alone!
> And Mother might
> Not think it's right
> Without a chaperon!
> I might say something foolish.
> I might do something rash.
> I even might enjoy myself,
> So please, I've got to dash!

(*Turns, reacts with horror to what she's done, and
    DEBBY deftly drops padlock-key into her bosom,
    while she is singing:*)

DEBBY.
> Don't poop the party! Don't be a louse!
> Oh, Clarence, drat you,
> You're no statue!

Let's play house!
Your inhibitions must weigh a ton!
I've got no axe to grind!
Relax, you'll find it's fun!
(*sweeps him into the tango-rhythm, and they dance*)

[*NOTE: This is the business-setup of the song: While
one duo sings, the other duo dances, and vice-
versa.*]

PEGGY. (*has pried herself from* LORENZO'S *arms, and
circles wheel and signal-box, as he pursues, during:*)
Where is my code of ethics?
I can't be on the brink!
How could I have attempted this,
And what will people think?!
A harmless fling I termed it,
But there is no such thing!
If I mis-step, I'll wear my reputation in a sling!
    LORENZO.
            (*gets her hands, pulls her to him*)
*O mi bonita*! Love is a breeze!
A little wink,
A little drink,
A little squeeze!
Your reputation I'm sure will keep!
If people talk,
Say you were walking in your sleep!
            (*and back to:*)
    CLARENCE.
        (*free of* DEBBY, *back to her, arms folded*)
Don't taunt me with temptation!
I've heard of girls like you!
But, oh gee whiz,
The trouble is,
I don't know what to do!
I ought to put the brakes on,

And stop things where they are,
But, man alive,
I feel that I've already gone too far!
    DEBBY.
                *(arms about him from behind)*
Please won't you ask me for one more dance?
I'll acquiesce:
I wear a dress—
You wear the pants!
Forget your mother! This isn't sin!
And have no doubt
I won't give out that you gave in!

*(And this time they dance slowly, romantically, because
    music has slowed to insanely romantic ominousness
    as, on the bridge,* LORENZO *is melting* PEGGY'S
    resistance fast, and has her bent partway back over
    the signal-box, as she pleads fearfully:)*

    PEGGY.
I dare not do it!
    LORENZO.
*Mi amor*!
    PEGGY.
I'm sure I'd rue it!
    LORENZO.
*Por favor*!
There's nothing to it!
    PEGGY.
I implore you!
    LORENZO.
Let's pursue it!
    PEGGY.
Where's the door?!
I can't delay!
    LORENZO.
Don't be *passé* !

*(his lips are nearing her own)*

PEGGY.
I cannot play—
LORENZO.
Oh, please, I pray
You, say okay! . . .
*Olé* !

*(And as his lips zero in, her flailing hand drags at a signal-cord, and steamwhistle whoops, bells start ringing alarmingly everywhere, and lights black out on bridge, and:)*

CLARENCE. Hey! That's "Abandon Ship!"

DEBBY. We're *sinking*? Clarence, what'll we *do*?!

CLARENCE. Only one thing *to* do! I mean, what the hell, if we're gonna die, *anyway*—!

*(bends her backward into one hell of a clinch and kiss)*

DEBBY. *(getting her lips free)* Clarence, you picked a fine time to come to your senses! Don't you understand, you birdbrain?! We're going to drown! Let's get *out* of here! *(pulls free of him, vainly tries to yank door open)* Oh, good grief, I forgot about this! *(tugs frenziedly at knob in blind panic)*

CLARENCE. The key! Use the key! Remember? You've got the key!

DEBBY. *(fumbling and groping in bosom)* Clarence! I can't find it!

CLARENCE. *(now fully as panicky as she is)* What?! Here, let me help you look!

DEBBY. *(backing from him, terrified, palms pressed protectively to her cleavage)* Clarence! What are you doing?! No! Please! Stop!!! Wait a minute—!

CLARENCE. Hell, it wasn't *my* idea to act like a primitive!

*(He lunges for her, she screams, and her scream blends with loudening steamwhistle and bells, as lights*

*black out on her cabin, and that Promenade Deck backdrop comes swiftly down into place, and orchestra starts playing the racing, urgent, musical intro to:)*

### ACT TWO, SCENE SIX

*The Promenade Deck.* COUPLES *appear from left and right, in various stages of undress—pajamas, underwear, blankets, bath towels, etc.* PEGGY *and* LORENZO *will appear similarly—his tie is askew, hair mussed, cap missing, her gown perhaps with a dangling shoulder-strap—near left end of frightened* COUPLES. STEWARD *will be near center of stage, front.* HARRY, ANGELICA, DEBBY *and* CLARENCE *will enter and stay near right end of* COUPLES *during following song-start—*DEBBY *with a very messed-up outfit, and* CLARENCE *about the same as we last saw him,* ANGELICA *in robe, plus huge rollers in her hair, and* HARRY *in a neat suit and tie—except that he does not have his pants on—and is, despite this, wearing a fedora. But, from the moment* COUPLES *came onstage and the music reached its peak, they at once began to sing, huddled together in mutual terror:*

COUPLES.
We are sinking! We are sinking!
And we think it's rather stinking,
And our eyes are moistly blinking with despair, yet!
Though the Caribbean's glorious,
Its fish are predatory,
And they'll gulp us down before we get our hair wet!
Barracuda with ferocity,

Intent upon atrocity,
Leave expectations positively punk!
Now's the time to take up drinking,
For our confidence is shrinking,
'Cause it's certain if we're sinking we are sunk!
>    STEWARD.
Just a moment, folks! Do not expect the worst!
For your despair I know a few deterrents!
>    COUPLES. (*shout*) Tell us, quick!
>    STEWARD.
Since the sharks and such must be provoked at first,
Be still, and they won't sunder your concurrence!
>    COUPLES. Can't we kick?
>    STEWARD.
If you make a move, the sharks will disapprove,
And on your splashing limbs they'll surely sup!
>    COUPLES. What a fate!
>    STEWARD.
But I'm guaranteein', in the Caribbean,
If you drown serenely, they won't eat you up!
>    COUPLES. Ain't that great?!
>    HARRY/ANGELICA/DEBBY/CLARENCE.
S.O.S.! S.O.S.! How'd we get ourselves in such a
    mess?
What's the score? Where's the shore?
Treading water's such a beastly bore!
May we choose to refuse
To stand here at attention when we're shaking in our
    shoes?
Let's unite to say goodbye to
Our romantic Caribbean Cruise!

(*Then all three factions—*COUPLES, STEWARD, *and our
    forlorn quartet—re-sing their parts together in
    simultaneous and panic-stricken counterpoint to
    conclusion of number; then:*)

STEWARD. Now, remember, as soon as we find the lifeboats, it's women and children first!

(*All men—excepting* STEWARD *and* LORENZO—*instantly drop to their knees, clutching the hand of their companion-women like small children out with their mommies, while childishly sticking thumb of free hand into their mouths, and then ALL WOMEN and their "CHILDREN" take three short steps forward, eagerly, as* STEWARD *reacts with hands-on-hips disgust*)

Now, *really,* gentlemen!

(*As men give it up and get back on their feet,* ANGELICA *spots* LORENZO, *who is now pulling* PEGGY *toward center*)

ANGELICA. Lorenzo! What's happened? All those whistles and bells!

CLARENCE. Did we run into an iceberg?

LORENZO. (*with a scowl at* PEGGY) No—but *I* did!

HARRY. (*rushes to* PEGGY, *clutches her hand*) Peg, honey, are you all right? When the whistles sounded, and I didn't know where you were, the cabin was empty, I ran all over—! Hey—how come you look so rumpled and everything—?! (*glares suspiciously at* LORENZO) Just what's this guy been trying to pull?!

LORENZO. (*coldly*) Pull? *Senor* Tremayne, it was not *I* who pulled *anything*!

(*Stands back from* PEGGY, *becoming her accuser to the assembly, letting her stand there, slumped in gloom, like an Old Testament woman about to be stoned*)

This woman—it is *she* who pulled the signal-cord that stopped our engines! It is *she* who becalmed our ship! *She* who signalled a disaster! Do not think that it was *I* who brought you all here into the chill of the night! I had nothing to do with it! It was entirely the doing of *Senora* Peggy Tremayne!

HARRY. (*places arm across* PEGGY'S *shoulder*) Anything this lady does is perfectly fine with me.

PEGGY. Oh, Harry—! You *mean* that? After all I've—?

HARRY. Ssssh! There's nothing you could ever do that could change the way I feel about you. Not really. Oh, so maybe I blow my stack now and then, but it doesn't mean a thing—not where you're concerned.

(*Sings.*)

Sometimes, in the rush of things,
I turn and find I've never said
Many words to reveal
The things I conceal in my heart.
Sometimes, in the rush of things,
I find I've wasted time instead
With the business at hand,
And words that I've planned never start.

(COUPLES, STEWARD—*in fact, everybody else but*
    LORENZO—*will hum along and sway in rhythm as:*)

HARRY. (*continues*)

Sometimes I expect too much,
And give too little in return,
When all you want is a word, a touch,
Things I pray it isn't too late to learn.
But now, in the hush of things,
I'll trust my heart before my head,
So I won't be amiss
In telling you this is true:
I'm head-over-heels in love with you!

(PEGGY *goes into* HARRY'S *arms; meantime,* OFFICER
    *enters right, moves to* STEWARD, *and whispers in
    his ear*)

LORENZO. That's all very charming, *Senor* Tremayne, but the fact remains—this lady stopped our ship, turned off our engines in mid-voyage! We are all sitting here, immobile, and who do we have to thank for it? Your wife!

OFFICER. Absolutely! And *I* would like to be the first!

(*As* LORENZO *gapes,* OFFICER *solemnly shakes* PEGGY'S *hand*)

I thank you—my wife thanks you—my children thank you—

LORENZO. What are you doing?!

STEWARD. Sir, we just received a radio message from the Coast Guard. Our compass is malfunctioning and we're almost thirty degrees off course. If Mrs. Tremayne hadn't stopped the ship when she did, in five minutes more we would have torn out our bottom on the Tortuga Reef!

(*All react with mingled shock and relief*)

LORENZO. What?! Who is responsible for such carelessness! Who was on the bridge?!

STEWARD. Uh—sir—*you* were . . .

LORENZO. Uh. Oh. Yes.

(*Clears throat, starts to address* OTHERS)

Ladies and gentlemen, the danger is past. We will be under way shortly. You have nothing more to fear.

ANGELICA. No thanks to *you,* Lorenzo!

DEBBY. That's right! We're all safe and dry and alive, and, by your own admission, there's just one person responsible, and there she is!

MAN. Three cheers for Mrs. Tremayne!

ALL BUT LORENZO AND PEGGY. Hip-hip—Hurray! Hip-hip—HURRAY! Hip-hip—*HURRAY!*

(*Sing.*)

She saved us! She saved us! It's such a relief

To know that she saved us from wreck on the reef!
We might have been under the waves,
The tenants of watery graves!
We might have awakened to find we were dead!
We might have been feeding the fish, but instead,
We're safe, warm and dry, and the reason is plain:
Our hat's off to Mrs. Tremayne!

(COUPLES *converge upon* PEGGY *as music continues,
lift her to their shoulders, and carry her off, right,
and they—minus the remaining people—sing the
final bit of the song when the orchestra reaches that
point:*)

COUPLES.
We're safe, warm and dry, and the reason is plain:
Our love and our kisses, and thanks for our bliss is
What we owe to Mrs. Tremayne!

(COUPLES *and* PEGGY *are now off.* [*NOTE: This gives*
PEGGY *a chance to change for next scene;* HARRY,
*after all, has nothing to do but put on his pants.*])

ANGELICA. I'm *so* glad they walked off with her. It's
always such a letdown when the crowd tires out and
finally takes the person *off* their shoulders! (*turns to her
son*) Clarence, what have you done to that girl? She's
positively disheveled!

CLARENCE. She got kind of rumpled when I carried
her up on deck.

HARRY. Carried her?

DEBBY. I got so scared when the whistle sounded—I
guess I must have fainted.

CLARENCE. Luckily, I was calm enough to take advantage of the situation—

ANGELICA. (*eyebrows raised*) Oh? What did you do?

CLARENCE. (*rattled by all the turmoil, isn't thinking,
just talking*) The only thing I *could* do. I took off her
dress, and—

HARRY. (*very much the uncle/chaperon*) *You did what—?!*

CLARENCE. Wait, you don't understand! I had to find the key to the padlock!

HARRY. *What padlock?!*

CLARENCE. (*hides behind* DEBBY) Debby—tell him about the padlock!

DEBBY. (*almost does so, then thinks, then says brightly*) *What* padlock?

CLARENCE. (*seeing death in* HARRY'S *eyes*) Debbeeee!

DEBBY. Debby what?

CLARENCE. (*sags, gives in*) Debby . . . *darling.*

HARRY. You realize, of course, that you'll have to marry her?!

DEBBY. He's still in shock, Uncle Harry. But I'll explain things to him very slowly . . . !

(*goes into slow clinch with* CLARENCE, *who resists— then enjoys—and finally assists in*)

ANGELICA. (*back of wrist to forehead*) Oh, dear, this *is* a shock! Clarence—and Debby—it's all so sudden! (*takes deep breath, then drops wrist and smiles brightly*) Well, now that the shock's over, I guess I'll start writing out some wedding announcements! (*turns to still-unsuspecting* LORENZO) How do you spell your last name, Captain La Jolla?

LORENZO. *My* name? What are you speaking about? I thought you meant—

ANGELICA. Clarence is old enough to manage his *own* wedding. I am talking about *ours!*

LORENZO. Now, *uno momento, Senora* Bostick! If you are thinking for even the split of a second that I would—

ANGELICA. Lorenzo, who was absolutely derelict in his duty tonight?

LORENZO. Oh—well—it was this way—

ANGELICA. And who stands to lose his job if this dereliction is reported to the steamship company?

LORENZO. You do not mean—?

ANGELICA. And who—now, search your memory very carefully—who happens to be the *owner* of this steamship company . . . ? ? ?

LORENZO. (*after a long, exquisite pause of trapped-animal agony*) I seem to recall—the owner of the company is—(*gulps, then sighs*) The most ravishing woman I have ever set eyes on—?

ANGELICA. (*sliding triumphantly into his arms*) That'll do for starters! On your mark . . . get set . . .

LORENZO. (*sickly*) *Querida!*

ANGELICA. *Mi amor!* (*and it is **she** who bends **him** back in a mad Latin clinch*)

HARRY. Well, if you folks will excuse me—?
(ANGELICA/LORENZO *and* CLARENCE/DEBBY *are still happily embracing and kissing and paying him no heed at all*)
I think I'll go see where the crowd set Peggy down . . . I said, if you folks will excuse me—? . . . Well, whether you will or not—you've all just given me a terriffic idea! (*He exits happily in direction* COUPLES *took* PEGGY *off*)

OFFICER. (*studies still-clinching couples, then turns to* STEWARD) You know—all at once—I wish *you* were a beautiful woman—!

STEWARD. (*places his hand on* OFFICER'S *forearm*) You know—all at once—I'm awfully glad I'm *not!*

(*Turns and runs off, right, laughing;* OFFICER *glares after him, then shrugs and starts off in opposite direction; as he exits, quartet unclinches*)

DEBBY. (*starting off right, with* CLARENCE) Oh, Clarence, we're going to be so happy! Didn't I *tell* you life is just like in the movies?! Falling in love on shipboard! This is exactly as if we were in *An Affair to Remember*!

CLARENCE. (*smiles weakly*) Not to mention *The Poseidon Adventure*!

(*they exit*)

ANGELICA. (*towing* LORENZO *off left*) Now, come along, we have a million things to do! Our next port is San Juan, and I know a lovely little chapel there where we can be married as soon as we disembark!

LORENZO. (*fighting down to the wire*) But what if the chapel isn't available?

ANGELICA. Oh, it will be. I hold the mortgage!

(*She laughs gaily, and he rolls his eyes heavenward in despair as they exit, and backdrop rises on:*)


ACT TWO, SCENE SEVEN

*The Tremayne home, as at the top of the show.* PEGGY *and* HARRY *enter, each carrying two bags. She is in a beautiful travel outfit, but looks weary, and so does he. They set bags down in living room with a thud.*


HARRY. I'll get the rest of the stuff off the porch.

PEGGY. No—not yet—wait a moment. I just want to soak up this room. It's been so long. It's unspeakably marvelous to be back!

HARRY. I think you mean "unutterably." "Unspeakably" means "horribly."

PEGGY. (*laughs and goes happily into his arms*) Oh, you know what I mean!

HARRY. (*holding her fondly*) Do I ever!

BOTH. (*sing*)
Now at last it's over!
We're home again! Home again!
Far from all those silver lagoons!
Goodbye, guitars! So long, you stars!
Farewell to tropical moons!
Home again! We're home and
We'll nevermore roam again!
Though we loved our brief holiday,
Now that it has ended, we're happy to say:
We're home again, and home is where we'll stay!
          (*they dance, gently, contentedly; then:*)
Memories we've gathered, but now it's today . . .
We're home again, and home is where we'll stay!

(*As they finish,* MADGE *comes rushing in from front
     door, carrying a large bundle of mail*)

MADGE. Well, the world-weary travelers are back at
last! How'd it go, kids?
HARRY. Oh, it was—uh—really something!
PEGGY. It certainly was!
MADGE. Here, I've been stockpiling your mail. I
didn't think the mailbox was safe enough. A sneakthief
might come along and get away with all your overdue
bills!
PEGGY. (*laughs, takes bundle from* MADGE) Thanks.
If they're as bad as I think they are, I may just put a
"Thief Wanted" sign in the front window! (*starts sort-
ing through mail, reading casually, during:*)
MADGE. It must have been a ball, Harry. You look
ten years younger. Of course, at your age, that's not
saying much!
HARRY. It was an experience, all right!

(PEGGY *will continue reading envelopes, and discarding
     those already read onto armchair, during:*)

MADGE. Well, for Debby's sake, I'm sure glad you two could go. You know how it is, a young impressionable girl off in the romantic tropics without a chaperon! No telling *what* might have happened. But as long as she was with two mature, responsible adults, my heart could rest easy. . . . Say, where *is* Debby, anyhow?

PEGGY. (*without even looking up from mail*) On her honeymoon.

MADGE. (*jaw agape, sags back onto* HARRY, *who calmly supports her*) What? Peg—you're joking—no—you're *not* joking—Harry—this is awful—what were you two thinking of—my little girl—what will Henry say—how can I face him and tell him that she—that you—?!

HARRY. Now-now, Madge, it's all right.

MADGE. *All right*?! My only daughter's married a man I've never even met, and you say it's all right?!

PEGGY. (*looks briefly up from mail*) Oh, I'm sure you'll like Clarence when you meet him. (*returns to looking at mail*)

MADGE. "Clarence"?! Peggy, I don't even like his *name*! How did it happen? When did they meet? Why did you let them? Who *is* this guy, anyhow?!

HARRY. Clarence is the heir to sixty million dollars.

MADGE. (*straightens up instantly*) I always did like the name "Clarence." Wow, wait'll I tell Henry! Wait'll I tell the neighbors! Wait'll I tell my *bridge club*! *Wheee*! (*turns and dashes out front door*)

PEGGY. (*still sorting*) I *told* you it would be simple.

HARRY. I wouldn't have believed it till I saw it! She didn't even ask his last name!

PEGGY. She will.

MADGE. (*gallops back into room*) Does my brand-new son-in-law have a last name?

PEGGY. Of course.

MADGE. Oh, good! (*gallops out*)

HARRY. I have the feeling she'll be back again!

MADGE. (*galloping back in again*) Harry—?

HARRY. "Bostick"!

MADGE. (*does not pause in her gallop, but simply swings around* HARRY *like a horse coming around the turn, and will go galloping right out again as she says:*) Thanks!

HARRY. Of all the bubble-brained—!

PEGGY. (*reacts to envelope*) Oh, no! (*drops all other mail to floor, starts opening envelope*) I don't believe it—it can't be—! (*looks at letter, then drops that arm to her side, covers her eyes with her free hand, and then thrusts letter-holding hand from her side toward* HARRY) Brace yourself, honey.

HARRY. (*takes letter, looks at it, gapes*) Oh, no! It says that we—that we—

PEGGY. Have just won an all-expense-paid Caribbean Cruise for two! Talk about totally insane timing!

HARRY. Shall *I* tear it up, or do *you* want to?

PEGGY. Let's do it together! (*they each take an edge of the letter at top and bottom*) On your mark—

HARRY. Get set—

PEGGY.

(*Opens her mouth to say operative word—then pauses —then looks at* HARRY—*then he looks at her—and then:*)

It's ridiculous, of course.

HARRY. Of course.

PEGGY. I mean—we just got *back*—!

HARRY. Home again! Home where our hearts are! Home where we belong!

PEGGY. Right! I was silly to think for a moment that—that—and yet—

(*starts to muse aloud in song:*)

Maybe we could do it . . .

Though we've just been through it . . .

HARRY.
It might suit us to a "T" . . .
   PEGGY.
Why do I want you
Beside me, just we two,
Beginning this new jubilee—?!
   HARRY.

       (*with more spirit, as tempo picks up*)
The kids could stay on with their grandma!
   PEGGY.
We'll write and explain it, somehow!
   HARRY.
So, what the hell, give me your hand, Ma!
       (*they do quick it's-a-deal shake, and:*)
And let's get the hell out of here right now!
   PEGGY.
Have we both gone loony?
   HARRY.
We're just too weak to neglect this opportunity!
   BOTH.

       (*with arms about each other's waist*)
Caribbean moon, you're gonna see us soon!
Just chalk it up to lunacy!
Though we know that our motives are hazy,
And there's ev'ry good reason to scoff—
Call it dumb—
   PEGGY.
Call it nuts—
   HARRY.
Call it crazy—
   BOTH.
Call it what you please,
But please don't call it off!

(*Over following, Both start grabbing up bags, and head-
   ing toward front door with bouncy strides:*)

PEGGY.
Homelife's a drag!
HARRY.
Grab ev'ry bag!
PEGGY.
Flag us a cab!
HARRY.
Who'll pay the tab?
PEGGY.
We'll find a way!
BOTH.
Let's not delay . . . !

(*Music soars to climax as they stride gaily out of the
room in high anticipation of a romantic future,
as—*)


## THE CURTAIN FALLS


### End of the Show

This musical has been especially designed for moving smoothly from scene to scene without hesitation, yet with a minimum of effort by the stage crew. There are only five "full" sets—that is, sets which extend upstage to the full playing-depth: 1) The Tremayne home, 2) The Tremayne stateroom, 3) The ship's dining room, 4) The ship's ballroom, and 5) The double-set of side-by-side ship's bridge and Debby's cabin. Ample time has been allowed for the replacement of these sets, according to the following stage-area allotments: Imagine, if you will, four areas from the lip of the stage to the extreme upstage playing-area. If your stage were 16 feet deep, each would occupy four feet of that depth. (This would be the ideal size, but a stage only 12 feet deep with three-foot similar areas will work.) Let us call these areas from the lip of the stage, A, B, C and D. [Note: As action moves upstage, set-wise, playing-area B naturally includes area A, C includes A and B, and D includes A, B and C.] Each of these areas is separated from the other by either a curtain, a drop as specified in the script, or even by a flat, if your fly-space can handle the rise of that flat as required. Now, then, the area-use per scene of the show, in order, will be: In ACT ONE:

Scene   1) The Tremayne home — D
Scene   2) The boarding pier — A
Scene   3) The Tremayne stateroom — D
Scene   4) The promenade deck — A
Scene   5) The ship's lounge — B
Scene   6) The ship's dining room — D
Scene   7) The marketplace — A

Scene  8) The ship's pharmacy — B
Scene  9) Entrance to the ballroom — A
Scene 10) The ballroom — D


ACT TWO:


Scene  1) The Tremayne stateroom — D
Scene  2) The "daydream sequence" — A
Scene  3) The stateroom — D
Scene  4) A corridor (or the promenade deck) — A
Scene  5) The bridge and the cabin — D
Scene  6) The deck (lifeboat or promenade) — A
Scene  7) The Tremayne home — D


As you can see, especially in that four-scene group in Act One, from scene 7 through scene 10, there is ample time and space for each new upstage setup to be in place when the downstage-of-it scene is being played. Done in this way, with the use of those projections described in the script, scene can follow scene in smooth sequence, without pause, and keep the show moving briskly.

# HERE'S HOW

## A Basic Stagecraft Book

**THOROUGHLY REVISED
AND ENLARGED**

by HERBERT V. HAKE

COVERING 59 topics on the essentials of stagecraft (13 of them brand new). *Here's How* meets a very real need in the educational theater. It gives to directors and others concerned with the technical aspects of play production a complete and graphic explanation of ways of handling fundamental stagecraft problems.

The book is exceptional on several counts. It not only treats every topic thoroughly, but does so in an easy-to-read style every layman can understand. Most important, it is prepared in such a way that for every topic there is a facing page of illustrations (original drawings and photographs)—thus giving the reader a complete graphic presentation of the topic along with the textual description of the topic.

Because of the large type, the large size of the pages (9″ x 12″), and the flexible metal binding, *Here's How* will lie flat when opened and can be laid on a workbench for a director to read while in a *standing* position.

## *Bible Herstory*

### PATRICIA MONTLEY

### (May Double.) Satire.

### 18 females—Bare Stage

**Bible Herstory,** a one-act feminist satire in six scenes featuring an all-woman cast. In "Paradise Abandoned," Eve convinces God not to stifle Her creativity just because She made a mistake in creating Adam. In "Noah's Ark-itect," Noah's wife and daughter prepare for the flood and "inspire" Noah to build a boat. "The Sacrifice of Sarah" shows Abraham's wife working on a theatrical project to save a lazy Isaac's life. In "Miriam in Labor," Moses' sister bargains with Pharaoh's daughter for better working conditions. In "Queen Solomon and the Paternity Suit," her Majesty proposes to cut in half a philandering charioteer claimed by both wife and mistress. In "The Renunciation," Mary rejects the Angel Gabriella's offer of the saviorship of the world, but agrees to have a son.

### (Royalty, $20-$15.)

---

# Out of Our Father's House

### Play with music. (All Groups.)

### BASED ON EVE MERRIAM'S

### *Growing Up Female in America: Ten Lives*

### 3 females play 6 roles
### Musicians—1 Interior

*Arranged for the stage by Paula Wagner, Jack Hofsiss and Eve Merriam. Music by Ruth Cawford Seeger adapted by Daniel Schrier. With additional music by Daniel Shrier and Marjorie Lipari.*

Taken entirely from diaries, journals and letters of the characters portrayed. They are a schoolgirl—founder of the Women's Suffrage Movement, an astronomer, a labor organizer, a minister, a doctor and a woman coming out of the Jewish ghetto. They are watched as they grow up, marry and bear children. They do not covet men's jobs, but when they want careers they are ostracized. A very moving play seen through the words and eyes of 19th century American women.
Write for information about music.

### (Royalty, $20-$15.)